Guide for Internationals

Culture, Communication, and ESL

Prentice Hall Series in Advanced Business Communication

Guide for Internationals

Culture, Communication, and ESL*

*English as a Second Language

Sana Reynolds
Consultant
Cross-Cultural Communication

Deborah Valentine
Goizueta Business School
Emory University

Mary Munter
Series Editor
Tuck School at Dartmouth College

PEARSON
Prentice Hall

Upper Saddle River, New Jersey 07458

Library of Congress Cataloging-in-Publication Data
Reynolds, Sana.
   Guide for internationals : culture, communication,
and ESL / Sana Reynolds, Deborah Valentine.
      p. cm. -- (Prentice hall series in advanced business communication)
   Includes bibliographical references and index.
   ISBN 0-13-170524-5 (pbk. : alk. paper)
    1. Study and teaching--English as a second language.   2. Intercultural communication--
Handbooks, manuals, etc.   3. Business communication--Cross-cultural studies.   4. Corporate
culture--Cross-cultural studies.   5. Social values--Cross-cultural studies.   6. English language--
Foreign speakers.   I. Valentine, Deborah.   II. Title.   III. Prentice-Hall guides to advanced
business communication.
   HD8081.A5R49 2006
   650.1--dc22   2005003196

Acquisitions Editor: Ashley Santora
VP/Editorial Director: Jeff Shelstad
Associate Director of Production: Judy
  Leale
Production Editor: Marcela Boos
Manufacturing Buyer: Michelle Klein
Cover Art Director: Jayne Conte

Cover Design: Kiwi Design
Composition: Laserwords
Full-Service Project Management: Jennifer
  Welsch, BookMasters, Inc.
Printer/Binder: R.R. Donnelley–
  Harrisonburg
Typeface: 10.5/Times

Credits and acknowledgments borrowed from other sources and reproduced, with permission, in this textbook appear on appropriate page within text.

Pearson Education LTD.
Pearson Education Singapore, Pte. Ltd
Pearson Education, Canada, Ltd
Pearson Education–Japan
Pearson Education Australia PTY, Limited
Pearson Education North Asia Ltd
Pearson Educación de Mexico, S.A. de C.V.
Pearson Education Malaysia, Pte. Ltd

10 9 8 7 6 5 4 3 2 1
ISBN 0-13-170524-5

For Luke, whose faith in me makes all endeavors possible.

Sana Reynolds

To my international friends and students who provide endless inspiration.

Deborah Valentine

Contents

PART II
COMMUNICATING IN THE U.S. CULTURE · 33

PART III
WRITING REFERENCES FOR ESL 93

PART IV
RESOURCES FOR ESL 111

Introduction

As an international employee, you are part of a remarkable number—100 million people—living in the United States whose roots are in a culture other than Northern European. If you face communication challenges as an international, you are not alone. It is no simple matter to live and work in another country. You may have experienced a conflict between your natural inclination to do things the way you have always done them and the expectations of your managers that things be done the "American" way. This conflict can be profound because it touches the culture you brought with you when you came to the United States—ways of thinking, behaving, and communicating that are particular to your own culture. This conflict caused by the clash of cultures can be so difficult that it may prevent you from being as effective as you might be.

The purpose of this book is to help you bridge the gap between your native culture and that of the United States. Our goal is to reduce the discomfort caused by cultural clashes by providing specific information about American culture, workplaces, and business practices. Information on logistics, housing, schools, or services is outside the scope of this text. Rather, our concern is to help you succeed in living and working in the United States by understanding the U.S. culture and how it affects business communication.

HOW THIS BOOK CAN HELP

You may have experienced unhappiness or frustration with the conventions of American business. You may have found that you are undervalued even though your core competencies and technical skills are superior. You or someone you know may have experienced the following issues when dealing with American businesspeople:

- Difficulty knowing appropriate eye contact and gestures
- Uncertainty about using a direct or indirect style in communication
- Inability to make your points clear in meetings or in negotiations
- Hesitancy in presenting negative information
- Difficulty knowing how close to stand during conversations

If you plan to work in the United States in the future; if you have been puzzled by the beliefs, behaviors, and work ethic of your American managers and peers; if you wish to become a more successful communicator in your current job, this book can help by providing essential information about U.S. culture and workplace practices.

WHO CAN USE THIS BOOK

If you are interested in preparing yourself to live and work in the United States, wish to enhance your knowledge about American culture and business practice, or seek to improve communication with your American managers and customers, you will benefit from the information presented in the *Guide for Internationals.* Many groups will find this book useful:

- International managers, executives, and other business professionals who wish to communicate more effectively in the U.S. workplace
- International students pursuing MBAs and other graduate degrees (engineering, healthcare, etc.) who wish to work in the United States after graduation
- Instructors in both graduate and undergraduate ESL, EFL, and other communication courses who work with international students
- Corporate trainers who educate international workers about U.S. business culture and practices

WHY THIS BOOK WAS WRITTEN

We have taught thousands of international business professionals and MBA students at corporations and universities in the United States and abroad. Although many of them spoke excellent English, many were unprepared for the realities and demands of working successfully in the United States.

For example, we have trained many Chinese managers, who, despite excellent language skills, solid core competencies, and a sound knowledge of management theory, could not interact effectively with American managers because of their inability to establish appropriate eye contact or reluctance to actively participate in brainstorming sessions. We have worked with businessmen from the Middle East who were misunderstood by their American counterparts because of a lack of knowledge about acceptable body language and distance requirements.

As a busy international, you may not have the time to read multiple books that are often too long or academic. That's why Prentice Hall is publishing the Prentice Hall Series in Advanced Communication—brief, practical, reader-friendly guides for people who communicate in professional contexts. (See the inside front cover of this book for more information on the series.)

- *Brief:* The book summarizes key ideas only. Culling from thousands of pages of text and research, we have omitted bulky examples, cases, footnotes, exercises, and discussion questions. Instead, we offer guidelines that summarize cutting-edge research and real-life examples drawn from our business experience.

- *Practical:* This book offers clear, straightforward tools you can use. It includes only information you will find useful in a professional context.

- *Reader-friendly:* We provide a reader-friendly and easy-to-skim format using a direct, matter-of-fact style.

HOW THIS BOOK IS ORGANIZED

Part I: Understanding the U.S. Culture (Chapters 1–3)

Internationals who wish to communicate in the American workplace need to understand the way culture shapes communication. This section explores the way culture affects values, attitudes, and behaviors in the United States.

1. American Individualism
2. American Attitudes Toward Time
3. American Business Relationships

Part II: Communicating in the U.S. Culture (Chapters 4–7)

Even when everyone in a meeting speaks English, misunderstandings occur because of cultural expectations, idiomatic expressions, industry jargon, and untranslatable slang expressions. In this section, we analyze how Americans use language and how their expectations and preferences impact the success of your career.

4. Effective Writing
5. Powerful Presentations
6. Effective Nonverbal Communication
7. Western Negotiation

Part III: Writing References for ESL

Writing another language presents many challenges. You may not be acquainted with the acceptable formats used in U.S. business. Others may judge your ideas negatively because of faulty grammar, usage, or punctuation. This section provides a brief but useful handbook for quick and easy reference.

Part IV: Resources for ESL

The book ends with the following resources:

A. *Questionnaire for Self-Understanding*—a tool to develop personal awareness
B. *Online resources* for additional information and help (accent management, grammar tools, courses, ESL sites)
C. *Bibliography*—listing the sources that shaped the academic and research backdrop for our discussions
D. *Suggested novels* for learning about the U.S. culture
E. *Suggested Films* for learning about the U.S. culture

ACKNOWLEDGMENTS

This book would not have been possible without the knowledge we acquired during the past 20 years through consulting and teaching in the United States and overseas. Special thanks to our international clients, students, and colleagues at Avon Products, Bank of Boston, Bank Degang Negara, BellSouth, the Coca-Cola Company, the Central Bank of Kuwait, Esso/Exxon Hong Kong, the Federal Reserve Bank of New York, Goizueta Business School at Emory University, Hutchison Whampoa, IBM, the New York Times, Nippon Credit Bank, Pfizer Pharmaceuticals, Stern School of Business at New York University, and the University of Hong Kong.

Particular mention is due to Professor Mary Munter, our indefatigable reader and editor; Professors Victoria Badalamenti, Mary Nance-Tager, and Beth Pacheco, who combed our manuscript for slippages and omissions; Luke Reynolds, who helped compile our list of recommended films; our colleagues at the Association for Business Communication for their support; and our excellent team at Prentice Hall, especially David Parker.

But most of all, we acknowledge each other. We care deeply about our subject and hope our knowledge will help newcomers succeed in living and working in the United States.

Sana Reynolds
Cross-Cultural Communication Consultant
sreynold@stern.nyu.edu

Deborah Valentine
Goizueta Business School
Emory University
deborah_valentine@bus.emory.edu

PART I

Understanding the U.S. Culture

CHAPTER I OUTLINE

1. Origins of American individualism
2. Common American convictions
3. Individualism guidelines for internationals

CHAPTER I

American Individualism

The individual is the basic unit of nature.
—JOHN LOCKE

All human beings grapple with the definition of "self," thinking about who they are and how they define their place in the world. Despite this ability of all peoples to be self-reflective, Americans seem particularly focused on the self rather than on others— priding themselves on being independent, autonomous, self-reliant, risk-taking, assertive, responsible for their destinies, and accountable for their actions.

One of the first things many internationals notice about Americans is their individualism. Americans sometimes seem more concerned with themselves than with others—spending an inordinate amount of time and energy talking about themselves—and using the pronoun "I" to preface many statements and dominate many conversations.

An HR (Human Resources) director of a telecommunications firm in Seattle, Washington, complained about the overwhelming focus on the individual in a recent conversation with a communication consultant. "Some of the cover letters I receive use the personal pronoun 'I' fifteen times—and that's just in the first paragraph!" The HR director reported that division managers are currently looking for employees who work well in teams, so she advises people who are applying for jobs to use more of a team focus in their job search documents. "For some of these applicants, that's going to be a tough job."

To better understand the importance of individualism in American life and work, we will briefly discuss the origins of this belief and analyze the common convictions held by most Americans.

I. Origins of American individualism

Where does this focus on the self come from? A quick look at the religious, philosophical, and historical background that led to the doctrine of individualism can show why this preoccupation with the "self" has become a cornerstone of American culture.

Sources: Western individualism traces its origins from a variety of sources such as the theories of Greek philosophers, the Judeo-Christian tradition, the personal achievements of Renaissance artists, the explorers of the Age of Exploration, the political theorists of the French Revolution, and the thinkers of the Age of Enlightenment. The seventeenth-century English philosopher, John Locke explained the theory of individualism in his *Essay Concerning Human Understanding*. Locke argued that each individual is unique; that all values, rights, and duties originate in the individual; and that the interests of the individual should be paramount.

Proverbs: The English language abounds in proverbs confirming the value of individualism in the United States. The American ideal of individualism is a person who is independent ("Do your own thing"), shows personal initiative ("God helps those who help themselves"), and who is faithful to his or her own inner truth ("March to the sound of your own drum. Follow your dream"). Whether in history, literature, or art, individual freedom and individual achievement are the virtues that Americans glorify.

Role models: American role models—be they the cowboys, homesteaders, and fearless sheriffs of the Old West; the Carnegies, Rockefellers, or Gates, builders of immense corporate empires and wealth of mythic proportions; or the action heroes in today's movies, and video and computer games—are all depicted as lone agents who pursue their dreams and accomplish their goals with little or no assistance.

> *Even the U.S. Army emphasizes the role of the individual. Using its theme, "Army of One," in television recruiting ads, in their site on the Internet, and in printed publications, the concept is that "the strength of the Army lies not only in numbers, but also in the individual Soldier."*

The result is that most Americans believe that people have separate and unique identities, that they are responsible for their destinies, and that each person can make a distinct contribution to the world.

Childhood: Individualism is instilled in most American children shortly after birth, when they are put in a separate room immediately or after a few weeks or months. This goal is pursued throughout childhood, as American parents encourage children to make their own choices about food, clothing, and toys. When a particular choice doesn't work, the child experiences the results of the decision. ("You've made your bed, now lie in it.") The aim is to form self-reliant persons, capable of supporting themselves and living on their own. In fact, children who still live with their parents past the early twenties are viewed as immature.

> *"Where are you living now? Did you find an apartment?" I asked a young business associate, Hyun Kim. Korean-born, with a newly minted MBA degree, he looked uncomfortable at my question. "Please don't tell anyone, but I am living at home." So strong is the American ideal of the individual unencumbered by family, that my colleague was ashamed to admit he was living with his parents. In the more collective culture of his native Korea, his living arrangements would have been seen as both appropriate and prudent.*

Education: The U.S. educational system also fosters independence and individuality: in preschool and kindergarten, children participate in "show and tell" activities; in grammar and high school, adolescents ask questions and defend their opinions in individual presentations, class discussions, and debates; in college and university, a sizeable percentage of their grade reflects their participation in class. This public recognition of individual effort even extends to the teaching practice of selecting mistakes from the work of individual students and using them to present a specific point or illustrate a particular problem.

Careers: Launched on their careers, young Americans continue to experience affirmation of the value of having and expressing individual opinions and convictions and of competing with each other. Promotions are often painfully slow for the silent, the reserved, the thoughtful workers who prefer to deliberate before offering an opinion; others view them as uninvolved, uninterested, and lacking in commitment. The clear, direct, vociferous communicator, who maintains eye contact and aggressively offers an immediate response in meetings and brainstorming sessions, is rapidly promoted and seen as articulate and clear thinking—a leader. ("The squeaky wheel gets the grease.")

2. Common American convictions

This individualism leads most Americans to share the following widely held convictions:

Individual identities are more important than group identities. Americans tend to value their individual identities over their group identities. Although they may belong to many groups that influence specific behaviors or decisions (nuclear and extended family, religious affiliation, social clubs, professional organizations, parent associations, or support groups), it is the individual that tends to be the most important unit in the American culture; individual rights and needs usually take precedence over group rights and needs. The goal in the United States is to develop responsible citizens capable of making choices and assuming accountability for personal issues and problems.

- *Life decisions:* Professional and career choices, selection of marriage partners, and decisions about childrearing practices are normally made by the individual with independence as the life goal.
- *Impermanent relationships:* Many Americans view relationships as temporary contracts that can be broken whenever one party chooses. Even family relationships or intimate friendships may be severed if they threaten personal goals.

Equality is a sacred right.   Closely related to individualism is the value of equality—present in everything from government (the right to vote) and law (the right to a fair trial) to social relationships (preference for informality, the immediate use of first names as a social equalizer). Equality is defined as "inalienable" by the U.S. Declaration of Independence: "We hold these truths to be self-evident, that all People are created equal, that they are endowed by their Creator with certain unalienable Rights, that among these are Life, Liberty, and the Pursuit of Happiness." Equality of treatment is critical to allow each individual the fullest potential for personal growth. The American culture manifests a deep respect for the individual, one so profound that it may resist all limitations on personal freedoms, even those intended to preserve life.

> *Motorcycle helmets reduce injuries and save lives; therefore, most states have passed laws requiring the wearing of helmets by young people (ages 16 and under). Motorcycle advocacy groups, however, continue to fight for the right to be "free" of helmets.*

One website states, "We will see a return to the time when motor-cyclists were free to choose whether or not they wished to wear a helmet. Once again 'Freedom of the Road' will stand for something more than a distant memory."

Competition is necessary and desirable. Both the commitment to individualism and the equality necessary to achieve it are supported by a belief in the value of competition between people and groups. Competition is encouraged in the United States: children are encouraged to win, to "be number one"; adults are constantly ranked, graded, evaluated; institutions and companies compete for an ever-greater market share.

To maintain fairness and equality, and prevent the potential negative fallout from unbridled competition, Americans write detailed rules, laws, contracts, and elaborate agreements that clearly articulate the specific rights and duties of the concerned parties. Should disagreements arise, opposing parties achieve a solution through direct confrontation (arguments and rebuttals). The belief is that truth or justice will emerge from this "competition" between contrasting points of view. The quality of the evidence presented, the logic of the arguments, and the persuasive ability of the people involved will lead to a fair compromise. To enable resolution to happen, the American system of education emphasizes self-expression and assertiveness, and prizes the ability to articulate ideas clearly and eloquently.

Materialism is good. Most Americans consider it their right to be physically comfortable. They expect to have access to a large variety of foods; clothing for many occasions; sizable and comfortable homes equipped with the latest in labor or time-saving devices; reliable means of transportation; and a comfortable retirement. They view being materially well off as a symbol of success and often judge others by their material possessions.

Science and technology can solve most problems. Most Americans also believe that anything is possible when scientists, researchers, inventors, and engineers combine forces to work on a problem. From addressing personal trauma to exploring space, Americans trust science to find the answer.

This faith in science is grounded on two assumptions: that humans can control reality and that rational thought is powerful. This perception is deeply embedded in Western civilization: from Galileo to Locke, Descartes, Russell, and Einstein, Western cultures have long believed that most problems can be explained and solved by science.

The U.S. Office of International Affairs published a document that highlights this American belief. "Science, technology, and health aspects play a large role in a discussion of such critical topics as nuclear nonproliferation, use of outer space, population growth, adequate and safe food supply, climate change, infectious diseases, energy resources, and competitiveness of industrial technologies."

THE PERVASIVE ROLE OF SCIENCE,
TECHNOLOGY, AND HEALTH IN FOREIGN POLICY

Progress requires change.   Similar to their belief in science and technology, many Americans accept the need for change; they fervently believe that change leads to improvement and progress. They change themselves through plastic surgery, psychoanalysis, support groups, and self-help books (which consistently dominate best-seller lists). They change domiciles, easily moving for better career opportunities or a different lifestyle, even when it means moving away from family. They change the environment—clearing forests, draining swamps, moving mountains, and altering the course of rivers.

In general, Americans see new ideas and products as positive and embrace change as necessary and desirable—an inevitable accompaniment to progress. Although this enthusiasm for change can often translate into a continual search to reinvent oneself and one's friends or a love affair with fads, it also accounts for the ceaseless and often-admirable pursuit of social reform.

Work has intrinsic value.   Americans also value work. When meeting each other for the first time, members of other cultures may ask about family or group affiliation; Americans usually ask "What do you do?" Work is therefore seen, not only as the means to achieve financial stability or material comfort, but as a definition of who one is, of one's identity.

Space and privacy are important.   Most Americans have a greater physical space and privacy requirement than many other cultures. In fact, Americans value privacy so greatly that they have made it law: the fourth item in the Constitutional Bill of Rights guarantees all citizens the right to be secure in their persons, houses, papers, and effects against unreasonable search and seizure. This requirement for privacy can be seen in both business and personal environments:

- *In the home:* Individual bedrooms are considered essential. Privacy is considered critical to a peaceful family life.

- *In the office:* Private offices confer status. Closed doors signal a desire for privacy; entering without knocking is unacceptable.

- *In crowds:* Crowding is perceived as invasive, and when it is unavoidable—in subways, buses, elevators—strict guidelines (maintaining a rigid body, avoiding eye contact, facing the exit door) govern personal behavior.

Communication should be direct, explicit, and personal. Because they value individuality and independence, most Americans prefer direct and personal self-expression.

- *Direct explicit messages:* Americans expect communication to reflect the speaker or writer's views and appreciate clear, direct, and explicit communication.

- *Linear logic:* Like most individualist cultures with Western European roots, American logic emphasizes a linear, cause-and-effect thought pattern.

- *Personal accountability:* Messages are expected to capture personal opinion and express personal accountability. Thus, Americans may seem to "sell" themselves and assert their accomplishments; however, they also usually assume responsibility for mistakes.

Business should be competitive and focus on transactions. Just as competition is encouraged in U.S. education to produce the best result—the most articulate, independent thinker and communicator—it is also encouraged in business practice. Results, rather than the process, are paramount. The deal itself is paramount, rather than the relationship or context; business decisions are made by scrutinizing facts (such as due diligence, credit reports, and quarterly earnings) and technical competence (such as past experience and educational credentials).

- *Measurable results:* The focus of business is on results, and success is calculated by measurable results, such as quantifying profit or market share, controlling productivity, and analyzing the customer base.

- *Competitiveness:* Most Americans believe that competition ensures results. If results don't meet expectations, transactions can be cancelled and contracts can be broken.

- *Separation of personal and business life:* American business-people generally separate their professional and personal lives, the business deal from the relationship. The goal is the contract, the transaction, or the sale; the relationship is secondary and superficial, just cordial enough to do business. In fact, personal connections or relationships are often avoided; they are seen as granting an unfair advantage and interfering with objectivity.

Exceptions to the general rule: Although individualism is an invaluable tool in understanding the American culture, two caveats must be kept in mind.

1. *Subcultures and ethnic communities may cause value varia- tions.* Most culture have various subcultures that may influence how individuals define themselves. For example, many African Americans and Caribbean Americans live in extended family units and prize individual and collective values equally. Within each culture, different ethnic communities may display distinc- tive individual and collective values. Communities that retain group-oriented values, especially those promoting the solidar- ity of the extended family, include Native Americans, Middle-Eastern Americans, first- and second-generation Asian and Latino Americans, and Americans of Mediterranean descent.

2. *Gender may influence behavior.* In addition, various studies show distinct differences in how men and women espouse indi- vidualism. Women tend to value attachment, connection, and caring; men emphasize separation and self-empowerment.

INDIVIDUALISM GUIDELINES FOR INTERNATIONALS

Keep in mind the following guidelines based on American individuals.

When studying in the United States ...

- *Ask questions.* Understand that the American educational system encourages dialogue and debate.

- *Express your opinion.* Empower yourself to offer your ideas during discussions. Remember, a sizeable percentage of your final grade may depend on your participation in class. Being "right" is less important than playing an active role in class debates.

- *Communicate directly.* Prefer direct, clear, explicit messages using a linear, cause-and-effect thought pattern.

- *Don't be afraid to compete.* Unlike other cultures, U.S. education stresses the ability to work individually and compete with one another.

When working in the United States ...

- *Accept personal responsibility.* Understand that American businesses often reward individuals. Be willing to accept personal credit as well as accountability for successes and failures.

- *Respect space requirements.* Understand the American need for privacy. Always knock and wait to be invited before entering rooms or offices. Notice and imitate acceptable crowd behavior.

- *Focus on the transaction.* Understand that in the egalitarian world of American business, the most competitive bid will win over any existing relationship.

- *Use data and logic.* Appeal to competitiveness and equality and present facts, numbers, and statistics. Don't be afraid to use scientific and technical data. Construct your persuasive argument using linear, cause-and-effect logic.

- *Communicate directly.* Prefer direct, clear, explicit messages; indirect or unclear messages may cause discomfort and doubt.

CHAPTER 2 OUTLINE

1. What newcomers notice
2. American attitudes toward time
3. Time guidelines for internationals

CHAPTER 2

American Attitudes Toward Time

In America, an hour is forty minutes.
—GERMAN PROVERB

For many people coming to study or work in the United States, the rapid pace of life and the unrelenting emphasis on time can be challenging. Americans seem to be constantly rushing to get to their appointments or meetings. People eat quickly, in fast-food restaurants or even while driving or walking. They restlessly seek attention in stores and business offices in their efforts to complete errands during a lunch hour. They push past you on the street and get impatient when you don't match their rapid walking rhythm. They seek and value inventions and services that save time: from one-stop gas stations, microwave ovens, bulk shopping, prepared-food delivery, to ever faster computers and cars.

The constant restless motion of Americans startles many newcomers. Even small town or suburban environments, slower in their daily rhythms, are not impervious to the call for constant motion. In the more relaxed South or Midwest, for example, many small-town dwellers think nothing of driving 75–100 miles to work, to dine with a friend, or to enjoy an evening of music or theater.

1. What newcomers notice

For newcomers from more relaxed cultures who have been on sun, seasonal, or Circadian-rhythm time, the American mastery of time management with its panoply of calendars, daily planners, personal digital assistants (PDAs), alarm clocks, and watches can be daunting. For people from cultures that allow time to flow like a river or unfurl naturally, the American reliance on efficient and rigid scheduling seems unnatural. For those who adhere to the Chinese proverb "He who hurries cannot walk with dignity," Americans' harried personal rhythms can seem ludicrous. An Iraqi businesswoman captured this discomfort when she related this story:

> At home, if I wanted to go to the doctor, I walked to the doctor's office. If I wanted to visit a friend, I just went to visit. I didn't call and ask for an appointment or ask if my friend could come over two weeks from Friday at three o'clock. I am not used to the American custom of giving away time in the future. How can I know where I will be in two weeks and what I will want to be doing?

One of the ways to determine whether a belief is widely held is to examine the language for recurring proverbs and common expressions. The English language abounds in expressions that capture the idea of time as a precious entity:

> Time is money. Save time. Don't waste time. Use time wisely. Manage your time well. One thing at a time. A stitch in time saves nine. The early bird catches the worm. He who hesitates is lost. Strike while the iron is hot. Never put off to tomorrow what you can do today.

How does this approach to time affect the daily life of Americans? In the next section, we examine more closely the impact this attitude toward time has on how Americans live and conduct business.

2. How Americans behave

Americans, especially in the U.S. business culture, tend to follow a strictly linear interpretation of time, generally living and working by a linear clock. Most view time as a valuable commodity to be used, not wasted; a businessman from Tajikistan remarked, "Americans think it is a sin to do nothing." Most Americans work sequentially, concentrating on one thing at a time; this approach appears to them to be an efficient, impartial, and precise way of organizing life—especially business. Because of the strong belief in individualism and individual achievement Americans will try to pack as much as they can into every day.

What do all these generalizations mean in daily life? How do they influence human conduct? The following values are important to most Americans.

Live by schedules: Most Americans decide on and live by a daily schedule. Schedules are critical; they permit planning and prevent uncertainty. As the following example illustrates, many Americans value their PDAs or daily planners more than any other possession.

A police officer in New York City expressed surprise at the reactions of a young businesswoman whose purse was stolen on the subway. "She was much more upset by the loss of her Blackberry (PDA) than her wallet."

Measure time in small segments: Most U.S. businesspeople measure time in small units, and divide their daily schedules into 15–30 minute segments. They expect meetings to fit in that time frame, as the following comments made by a consultant from Mali attest:

I have learned that when an American with whom I am doing business looks at his watch, it means I am taking too much of his time and had better leave quickly. This usually happens after 20–25 minutes. This is very different from my culture where meetings will take however long they need to take.

Prize punctuality: American businesspeople dislike lateness, because it disrupts the schedule and affects all subsequent appointments. They prize punctuality and consider promptness a basic courtesy as well as a proof of commitment. Although you may be excused for being 5 minutes late for an appointment or meeting, being 15–30 minutes late will cause intense irritation and may be interpreted as contempt for the person or situation.

Complete one task at a time: Most American businesspeople are irritated by interruptions and expect complete concentration on the task at hand; doing two things at once (such as taking a telephone call during a meeting) is viewed as being inattentive or may even be considered rude.

> *Timothy Watson, a vice president at a prestigious engineering firm, had an appointment with Mr. Mahmoud, a Saudi official, at 10:00 AM to discuss a forthcoming project. He arrived at 9:45 and was kept waiting for more than an hour. When he was finally ushered into Mr. Mahmoud's office, he found several other people in the room.*
>
> *After serving coffee and engaging in seemingly endless small talk (interrupted frequently by calls on both the desk telephone and his cell phone), Mr. Mahmoud finally turned to the American and opened up the subject of his visit. Although Mr. Watson was eager to get on with serious discussions, he was hesitant; he was not sure of Mr. Mahmoud's complete attention.*

Target the short term: Not only do American businesspeople normally measure time in short periods, they usually plan for the short term and report earnings and profits in quarters. Expatriates working in Hong Kong, Singapore, and Malaysia often comment on the disparity between what their American and their Chinese managers value: American managers tend to measure return on investment by analyzing quarterly earnings; Chinese managers focus on building relationships and long-term equity. This difference in focus is captured metaphorically in the following quotation from *Nation's Business:*

> *Tatsuo Yoshida, former director of the Industrial Bank of Japan, stated that the Western business culture is like hunting, whereas in Japan, business is conducted more like rice farming. Japanese business focuses on the long-term; American businesses aim for immediate returns on investment.*

Value the future: Most Americans welcome change and innovation and constantly plan for the future. Their belief in the future is unshakeable: after all, the future promises greater expertise in controlling time and packing more into each time unit. Hence, U.S. businesspeople study time management to learn how to get more done every day.

> *Rana Rakesh, a native of India, moved to New York to become head of sales with an international computer company. She spoke English*

and three other languages fluently and was well trained in management and sales. After a few months in her new environment, however, Ms. Rakesh became extremely unhappy. "All these people do is rush about with their schedules in their hands," she complained. Ms. Rakesh's manager was very concerned, but for a different reason. He complained that she took too long on a given task. Indeed, he described her as "scattered" in her approach to the project schedules. His solution was to suggest that Ms. Rakesh sign up for a time management course. Ms. Rakesh's response was to resign.

Separate work and social time: Because many Americans plan and schedule nearly every activity in their day, it should come as no surprise that personal, family, and social activities are also scheduled. Most often, professional activities and business appointments are kept separate from time devoted to relaxation or interaction with family members. The overlap of work and family life described in the December 9, 2002, *New Yorker* is rare.

Mira Nair (director of the film Monsoon Wedding*) turned the final day of shooting into a sort of extended family outing. In addition to orchestrating cast, crew, and a platoon of extras, she was happily entertaining her son Zohran, Lydia Pilcher and her seven-year-old son, and Taraporevala, visiting from Bombay with her two young children. Far from distracting Nair, the swarming confusion seemed to intensify her concentration. "Her orientation to relationships is very familial. She doesn't work one task at a time or on a purely one-to-one basis. She creates groups," remarked her husband.*

Exceptions to the general rule: Although the concept of linear time is an invaluable tool in understanding the American culture, variations within subcultures and ethnic communities are notable. Subcultures and ethnic communities may use time differently from the dominant culture. Most Native American languages do not have words for "minute" or "hour." Mexican Americans frequently speak of "Latino time" when their use of time differs from that of the dominant culture. Hawaiians have "Hawaiian time," and Americans from Guam, the Philippines, and Samoa use the expression "coconut time" when referring to a relaxed and informal lifestyle ("The coconuts will fall when the time is right").

TIME GUIDELINES
FOR INTERNATIONALS

How does linear time impact studying or working in the United States, or transacting business with U.S. businesspeople? The following guidelines should help.

- *Respect schedules and value punctuality.* Be prompt for appointments: keeping a person waiting for 5 minutes is excusable, a wait of 15 minutes or more will cause annoyance. Tardiness is often regarded as a characteristic of the undisciplined or disorganized.

- *Use time efficiently.* Most Americans measure time in small units. Understand that you will have a brief period to make your point: most American professors and businesspeople schedule their days in 15 to 30-minute increments.

- *Focus on the conversation or meeting.* Don't answer your cell phone, read the newspaper, or perform any other task during a meeting or a brainstorming session. Remember that Americans expect your full attention; they may interpret multitasking as disrespectful and a lack of commitment to the goal.

- *Target the short term.* Americans expect objective data and analyses that address immediate or near-future gains and issues.

- *Focus on the future.* Americans prefer information that analyzes the present and predicts the future. Although some attention is paid to the past or the background surrounding a particular issue, information that focuses solely on the past is normally treated with impatience; it will be valued only if it casts light on future behavior.

- *Separate professional issues from personal concerns.* Many Americans are uncomfortable when personal reasons are given for professional problems or slippages. Stay away from revealing personal details; offer objective and concrete reasons for academic or business issues instead. Also, avoid having children in the office; Americans generally keep their personal and professional lives separate.

- *Value time.* U.S. businesspeople tend to be impatient: they view time as a precious commodity. To avoid potential misunderstanding, estimate the length of time required for a decision or a task, build in "wiggle room" (consider doubling the estimate), and give a precise date by which an answer will be ready.

CHAPTER 3 OUTLINE

1. The influence of power distance
2. Democratic social structures
3. Democratic business structures
4. Employer-employee relationships
5. Relationship guidelines for internationals

CHAPTER 3

American Business Relationships

> If liberty and equality, are chiefly found in democracy,
> they will be best attained when all persons alike
> share in the government.
> —ARISTOTLE

The rugged individual that is the American ideal demands a voice in government, a voice in business, and a voice in the church and community. Therefore, you will not be surprised to find that American business relationships are pluralistic and egalitarian.

In this chapter, we examine these relationships including power distance, democratic social and business structures, and employer-employee relationships. As an international, you will find the final guidelines useful as you prepare to communicate with Americans.

1. The influence of power distance

Dutch researcher Geert Hofstede defines "power distance" as the communication distance between the most and least powerful individuals within an organization. Not surprisingly, cultures with high power distance (such as Mexico, India, and Japan) may require that messages flow through channels. The U.S. culture, however, values less autocratic communication structures where messages can flow upward in the organization and where any individual can communicate directly without requiring a mediator.

Materials engineer Mohammed Jasim Ali worked for a transportation company in Chicago. Because he was from Indonesia, a high power distance culture, he often hesitated to make suggestions to his managers. The company started a mentoring program for international employees with interesting results. John Rice spent a few hours each week talking with Mohammed and advising him on career strategies. When Mohammed discussed his idea for a new type of container insulation, John strongly encouraged him to send the proposal directly to his division manager. Although Mohammed was reluctant, he followed John's advice. The company eventually installed the new insulation, which resulted in a savings of over $1 million in the first six months. In addition to praising his technical expertise, Mohammed's performance evaluation noted his "strong communication skills."

Preference for first names: Because power distance in the United States is low, employees sometimes use first names without titles. You will notice, however, that the use of first names varies in the United States, depending on the corporate culture.

- *Last names:* Use last names (family names) until you understand the corporate culture.
- *First names:* Use first names (given names) when invited to do so and always reciprocate.

Debra Alderman worked for Texas Instruments in the 1970s when most corporations tended to be more hierarchical and formal. At the time, Texas Instruments had a unique corporate culture. Rather than job description, color-coded identification badges indicated seniority. A green badge meant that the employee had worked for the company for less than one year. Silver and gold badges carried the highest seniority and were awarded to those who had been with the company for 10 or 20 years. Fresh out of college with an undergraduate degree, Debra was asked to call her division manager by his first name, Larry. Furthermore, Larry wore a green badge—the same color she wore. Even though he was older and more experienced, the company showed that it valued each of them equally. Debra later described her time at Texas Instruments as "empowering."

Preference for transparency: Along with low power distance comes the expectation for "transparent"—that is, open and clear—communication. In the U.S., publicly owned corporations, as well as government organizations, are supposed to communicate openly in their decision-making processes. The U.S. Securities and Exchange Commission (SEC) and other government organizations require clear communication and "plain English" in company documents. When you communicate with someone from the American culture, you will be more successful if you are aware of this American preference for clear and open information.

2. How Americans behave

In addition to low power distance, the U.S. business relationships are also influenced by democratic social structures—such as those regarding gender, rank and age, class, race, and religion.

Gender: The value of the individual, the ethic of hard work, and a low power distance would indicate to most internationals that America is a relatively work-friendly place for women.

> *In the last century, events during World War II propelled many American women into their first jobs. Today, more than half of all women in the U.S. work outside the home. A popular icon of the strong, independent American woman is "Rosie the Riveter," a poster character from the 1940s based on a song of the same title. By 1945, 6 million women worked in factories supporting the United States during World War II. This number represented a huge cultural shift with an increase from 20 percent to 36 percent of women in the United States employed outside the home. "Women did more than build weapons: they carved out powerful new roles for women in American society and opened doors for the generations of women to come."*
>
> —K. KNAUER
> *WHEN AMERICA WENT TO WAR,
> AMERICAN WOMEN WENT TO WORK*

You should be aware that U.S. laws protect employees from sexual harassment and gender discrimination. Almost all sexual harassment and gender discrimination involve offenses against women, but U.S. law provides protection for men as well.

- *Sexual harassment:* Most U.S. companies provide clear guidelines on what constitutes sexual harassment, which can include touching, fondling, or other unwelcome advances. It can also involve telling sexually oriented jokes, showing pornographic photos, or creating a hostile work environment.

- *Gender discrimination:* Gender discrimination means that a qualified person was overlooked for promotion in favor of the other gender. These laws also mandate equal pay for equal work.

Age and rank: Because America is reputed to be the land of equal opportunity, the relative age of a person is not necessarily an indicator of rank or position within the company. Older and more experienced workers may hold positions of responsibility, but not always. It is fairly common for a younger person to be hired or promoted as manager over older and more experienced individuals. In U.S. business, do not assume older people are senior to those who are younger; address everyone as an equal until you can properly identify those in positions of authority.

Social class: Based on its historical embrace of opportunity for all, Americans are free to move between social classes. In exclusive golf clubs, for example, net worth is usually more important for membership than family connections. As an international, you may be accepted as long as you can afford the initiation and monthly dues. Americans are also free to marry anyone they choose even if that person is from a different social class.

Race: Although the American ideal is that "all men are created equal," you probably know that the United States has endured difficulties in its relationships and fairness to those of other races. Now protected by law, American minorities have made tremendous strides in education, employment, and wealth. Each ethnicity brought cultural variations to the United States, and in some cases these variations have increasingly become woven into the fabric of American life.

Religion: In addition to separation of church and state, Americans also believe in religious pluralism. Internationals need to know that no state religion exists in the United States. Each person is free to devise his or her own personal identity and the relationship of that identity to a supreme being. Any group in the United States can form a church with protection by law and exemption from taxes.

In spite of some setbacks such as the burning of African American churches in the South, America remains a place where people of all faiths and all ethnicities work side-by-side on common goals and projects. The well-informed international businessperson should be aware of the following issues relating to religion.

- *Religious discussions:* Avoid discussing your religion on the job.
- *Time off:* If you must ask for time off for religious purposes, do your best to complete your work on time in consideration of your coworkers.

- *Employee accommodations:* Feel free to ask the employer for accommodations to your religion such as dietary requirements or space for daily prayers. These accommodations are guaranteed to you by law.

Education: Many Americans tend to distrust someone who has advanced education. The American ideal is that all topics should be discussed on a level understood by everyone and that people shouldn't flaunt their intelligence or education. Talk radio hosts love to rant about "pointy-headed intellectuals" and blame them for all the evils of the world.

Ample evidence for American anti-intellectualism appears in American literature. Washington Irving portrayed two archetypical American characters in his well-known story, "The Legend of Sleepy Hollow." Ichabod Crane is the gawky, thin, bespectacled schoolteacher, and Bram Bones is the strong, handsome laborer. They are both in love with Katrina, the farmer's daughter. In this American legend as in many others, Bram Bones outwits the schoolteacher and gets the girl in the end.

Most Americans are not looking for intellectual stars. They tend to look for someone with whom they can identify. They want leaders who are just "plain folks." Even highly educated and otherwise intellectual candidates for public office will take care not to appear better educated than their constituencies.

3. Democratic business structures

Like its social structures, American business structures are also democratic.

Dress: Those from other cultures are advised to observe dress norms in corporations carefully. Anyone who dresses too formally or too informally will be subject to criticism and mistrust. You may even hear Americans apologizing for wearing a suit when business casual attire is usually worn: "The reason I'm so dressed up is that I'm meeting a client for lunch." The ideal for most traditional corporations is to wear clothing that does not draw undue attention. Exceptions to this norm include segments of the fashion and entertainment business.

Office spaces: Large individual offices are the American ideal. Such offices provide plenty of room for personal expression and indicate that the employee has reached a position of respect within the organization. Officers of a large corporation typically enjoy a well-appointed office space with windows opening on a vast cityscape. However, even these individuals may be seen walking around the open office areas and chatting with employees of all job descriptions. The usual expectation is that office space will not interfere with free-flowing communication.

- *Office cubicles:* Many employees have a small space with a computer, telephone, and partial foam partitions. Even though employees can overhear phone conversations in the next cubicle, the partitions provide a semblance of individual space.

- *Equal space:* Many corporations in the United States provide their middle managers with a similar space to those they lead, thus demonstrating the great American ideal of equality.

Teams: Even in an extremely individualistic business culture as the United States, teamwork is important. The approach to teamwork in America, however, reveals much about the culture. The following steps show how a typical team functions in the United States.

1. Meet to determine the individual tasks to be accomplished.
2. Assign each task to a team member and set a schedule for completion.

3. Work independently on tasks.

4. Meet to report on progress.

Individuals within the team usually want project managers to know what segment of the team-task they accomplished. They experience a sense of "ownership" of that particular task and want to be recognized for their individual contribution.

Coaches of American professional basketball teams have the perennial problem of dealing with star players. Instead of team statistics, the U.S. culture demands individual statistics for each player. Each team member negotiates separately for salary based on individual statistics rather than team success. Individualism was a factor even in the summer Olympic games in Athens, Greece, where the U.S. 400-meter relay team failed to win the gold medal in spite of superior individual talent. The team had trouble with their baton exchanges. Asked by media representatives how many times they had practiced the baton exchange, the team admitted they had practiced only twice because, as Maurice Green stated, "We were busy practicing for our individual events."

4. Employer-employee relationships

In this section, we discuss another important set of business relationships: those of employers and employees.

The U.S. attitude toward employees is known as "mechanistic": tasks are more important than relationships and the worker is seen as a replaceable part in a machine. (In contrast, in other cultures, the attitude is "humanistic": relationships are more important than tasks, and the worker is seen as part of a company family.) Therefore, American employees feel little allegiance to the corporation and will resign if a better opportunity arises. Loyalty to a corporation is temporary, and the employee is free to move from company to company and job to job with no penalty.

> *President and CEO of Tower Automotive, Kathleen Ligocki's career demonstrates the mechanistic nature of American employment. In her twenty-plus years of work experience, Ligocki has held positions ranging from factory supervisor, to sales executive, to vice president for a succession of auto companies: General Motors, Ford Motor Company, and Tower Automotive. When she decided to leave her job, her boss encouraged her to stay, but said he "understood that this was a great opportunity for her to run a publicly traded company." The job experience was seen as more important than loyalty to any one company.*

A current term used to designate employees is "human capital," with the implication that the worth of the people who work for a company can be measured similarly to the worth of stocks, real estate, or other property.

> *Even the U.S. government's human resource agency, the Office for Personnel Management (OPM), has adopted the term "human capital." The OPM website states that sound investment in human capital is essential if agencies are to achieve their missions. OPM released a Human Capital Scorecard in 2001 to focus and support the human capital efforts of the agency.*

Advantages to mechanistic view of employees: Seeing the employee as a "position" rather than a "person" results in some financial advantages for U.S. companies.

- *Completing the deal:* In doing business with a U.S. corporation, you may discuss a business deal with the manager of the parts department. The person who holds that job may change in the middle of the transaction, but in most cases, the sale will still be completed.

- *Firing unproductive employees:* Because the task takes precedence over the relationship, firing unproductive employees is a common practice in the United States.

Disadvantages to mechanistic view of employees: The view of the employee as a machine part preserves the extreme individuality valued by the American culture, but it can also pose problems.

- *Adversarial relationships:* Because the mechanistic view of the employee-employer relationship focuses on the task over the relationship, it can create conflict between management and workers.
- *Arbitrary job loss:* Early in the previous century, laborers found that they needed to form unions to avoid what they deemed to be arbitrary job losses. Laws now protect Americans from unfair dismissal due to age, gender, or disability.

RELATIONSHIP GUIDELINES FOR INTERNATIONALS

Keep in mind the following guidelines.

Understand the impact of power distance on U.S. business.

- Find a mentor who can advise you about democratic relationships in your place of work.
- Recognize that low power distance in the United States may enable you to suggest ideas directly to the decision maker.
- Expect that first names may be used rather than titles and last names. If someone invites you to call them by a first name, you should reciprocate.

Examine democratic social structures in the United States.

- Be aware of gender discrimination and sexual harassment rules.
- Avoid sexual or ethnic jokes in the workplace.
- Keep your hands to yourself until you know the accepted greeting and hand-shaking routines of your office.
- Avoid discussing religion while on the job.
- Remember that a younger person may have the higher status.
- Treat everyone as an equal regardless of social class or race. Be respectful of all employees even if your job is more important.

Examine democratic business structures in the United States.

- Wear attire that is similar to your business associates. Select clean, well-pressed clothing that does not draw attention.
- Be aware that office size does not necessarily indicate rank.
- Because teamwork may have a different meaning, ask questions about the team's objectives and your role as an individual team member.

Be aware of the employer-employee relationship.

- Since employees change jobs frequently, the players may change in the middle of a transaction.
- Know that employer-employee relationships may be adversarial.

PART II

Communicating in the U.S. Culture

CHAPTER 4 OUTLINE

1. Addressing reader needs
2. Planning your document
3. Making your document reader-friendly
4. Eliminating errors
5. Using common business formats
6. Writing guidelines for internationals

CHAPTER 4

Effective Writing

The pen wounds deeper than an arrow.
—YIDDISH PROVERB

American business communicators often choose writing as a preferred communication channel. Why is writing considered important in the United States, especially in American business? Why should you pay attention to writing? Three reasons immediately come to mind:

1. Writing helps you clarify your thinking.

2. Writing is one of the best ways to share your expertise, your analysis, and your insights. Thus, your writing ability can be vital to your success in the U.S. business world.

3. As business organizations become more complex in the often-litigious U.S. business environment, clear writing becomes even more critical in the face of increased government regulation and the threat of consumer lawsuits.

However, good business writing differs from good general writing. Business writing has one overriding purpose: to transmit information rapidly and effectively for action by the reader. This task is more complicated than simply putting your ideas on paper in a clear and understandable manner. It means moving your ideas through the organization so that people will act on them. In other words, all forms of written communication in U.S. business must be seen as tools enabling readers to do their work, managers to make decisions, and customers to take action.

For writing to become a tool for readers, it must be organized to answer reader questions and address reader needs.

I. Addressing reader needs

The challenge of producing writing that transmits information and motivates action can only be met by examining and understanding the needs and concerns of American business readers. In today's world, where the Internet has caused available information to increase exponentially, and where corporate reengineering has meant a heavier workload for most people, readers are impatient to grasp immediately the message you're trying to transmit in your writing.

Most readers will have several specific questions as they open your document, questions such as: Why am I reading? How does this information affect me and my work? What is the importance of this document?

To maintain the interest of American business readers, you must answer these questions immediately by

1. Opening with a descriptive subject line and a clear purpose statement that preview the total message contained within your document,

2. Constructing your document with logic that matches the thinking of your audience,

3. Designing your document so that readers can locate important information "at a glance," and

4. Presenting information and data useful to the reader in a positive tone. Your document must be easy to read and free of error.

The next three sections discuss how to accomplish these goals.

2. Planning your document

The key to developing strategy and writing effective business documents for U.S. readers is planning before writing. You are writing to persuade your reader to act; the more thought you give to purpose, the more time you devote to planning, the greater the chance that your document will capture your research and insights and point the way to the necessary decision and action.

Balancing writer and reader needs: To become sensitive to the needs of readers and to make your analysis meaningful, you must realize that you are juggling two worlds when you write: your world and the reader's world. These worlds—writer/reader and purpose/response— become more balanced when you review, rethink, and sort the information for your reader.

Transforming information: Information you own as part of your profession or that you have gathered from your research or analysis must be transformed to be useful for your reader, because it is the reader, not the writer, who ultimately judges clarity of meaning and usefulness of information. It means writing for your reader, not for yourself, and viewing your document as a dialogue, not a monologue.

Remember to transform information that you have obtained through your research by translating your findings into your own words. Because the United States has strict laws prohibiting plagiarism, information obtained from other sources must either be surrounded by quotation marks or be paraphrased.

Grouping ideas: How will you tell your story? How will you arrange the ideas you want to share with your reader? To be effective, your thoughts must be grouped and arranged in a form the reader can understand and accept. Use empathy to put yourself in the reader's place, see your document from the reader's point of view, and shape it to inform the reader.

Creating a writing map: How?   Make a list of all of your ideas and then prioritize your list by asking which ideas are important, which support, and which are relatively unimportant. As you prioritize, look for sequence, connections, and patterns. Arrange your ideas into a flow that seems natural—that answers readers' questions and leads them comfortably from point to point.

What you now have is a "map"—an outline of the ideas you will develop in your document. The outline is for the writer what a blueprint is for an architect or a sewing pattern is for a tailor. Constructing the outline forces you to think through your ideas and put them in order.

Creating a writing map: Why?   Why is preparing a map or an outline important when writing business documents? Outlining reduces the chances of omitting essential information and allows you to correct gaps in logic, delete unnecessary repetition of ideas, or spot the presence of tangential material. It is much easier to catch these weaknesses in the outline than in the final draft. More importantly, outlining provides you with the opportunity to go beyond the surface, to think about your content from the perspective of your reader, and to make your analysis and discussion truly helpful for your reader.

Choosing a logical pattern: Once you've jotted down the ideas you want to cover in your document, decide on the best way to share those ideas with your reader—the logical pattern that captures and groups your thoughts. The common patterns include the following:

- *Time:* Arranging ideas in chronological order
- *Space:* Using geography or space to present your ideas
- *Essential elements:* The logical divisions of a larger topic
- *Problem/analysis/solution:* The issue, why it exists, how to address it
- *Order of importance:* Proceeding from the most important to the least important
- *Cause-and-effect:* What caused an event to occur
- *Deduction:* Main point followed by specifics
- *Induction:* Specifics leading to the main point
- *Control:* Comparing a situation to a standard
- *Pairing:* Questions/answers, pros/cons, advantages/disadvantages
- *Journalistic sequence:* Identifying who, what, where, when, why, and how

3. Making your document reader-friendly

In today's world of "information overload," making your document accessible and easy to read may mean the difference between being read and being ignored. The techniques that ensure reader-friendliness are descriptive subject lines, complete purpose openings, thoughtful visual layout, and an accessible dynamic style.

Subject lines and purpose openings: Two tools are available to you to identify purpose and preview content—the subject line and the purpose opening. The subject line should be specific and descriptive, clearly capturing the essence of the ideas you plan to elaborate.

Ineffective subject lines: vague and nonspecific

Accounting

Chemical Production in Texas

Effective subject lines: specific and descriptive

Unusual Accounting Practices in Our Indonesian Subsidiary

Texas Leads Nation in Chemical Production

The purpose opening should provide a snapshot of the entire document by including a preview of the total content and how that content is organized.

Ineffective purpose opening: does not preview total content

The purpose of this report is to present the results of our inspection of the 55 Water Street office for security vulnerability.

Effective purpose opening: previews report content and organization

This report describes the five security vulnerabilities found at the 55 Water Street office, analyzes the risk hazards of each, and recommends corrective action.

Visual layout: Remember that American readers value time: your goal is to make your readers understand exactly what you have to say—and understand it as quickly and as completely as possible. Careful visual layout allows the reader to grasp the essential message "at a glance" by displaying key ideas and using headings, subheadings, listings, and graphics to communicate dynamically. When you use thoughtful visual layout, busy readers can scan, skim, and spot-read.

A useful way to think about visual layout is to consider the role of sound and silence in oral communications. Just as oral communication is composed of words and pauses to allow response, a written document has two essential ingredients: words and the white space around them. This space should be used wisely because, without it, writing becomes a breathless, self-centered monologue, roaring down the page at breakneck speed, and discouraging the reader.

To design thoughtful, reader-friendly documents for American business audiences, consider these five questions:

1. *Would you want to read this document* if you were the reader? Or is the information presented in solid, forbidding blocks of text? Does your visual layout permit reading "at a glance"?

2. *What is the main point?* If your reader remembers only one thing, what must it be? Have you emphasized your main point so that your reader cannot miss it? If you present several key ideas, how do you signal them to your reader? Are you using lists, headings, bolding, etc.?

3. *Have you prepared your reader* for the information or data you present in your document? Do you preview your ideas in your opening and does your opening parallel the structure of your document?

4. *What about numerical information or statistical data?* Would it be easier for your reader if you grouped this information and presented it visually? Have you considered using a chart, a table, a graph?

5. *Does your document require a response?* Have you emphasized the necessary action and the date by which action is required? Have you made the response easy for your reader?

Dynamic style: Documents are considered reader-friendly if they are written in a dynamic and accessible style using simple, concrete words; short, powerful sentences; and small, bite-sized paragraphs. If you have planned your document, considered the best way to "tell your story," and thought about visual layout, you will probably know what thought goes into every sentence slot. You can now concentrate on phrasing the shortest, simplest, most powerful sentence that fits that slot.

Every sentence in a business document must be clear, concise, and free of jargon. Each word must contribute needed meaning or tone. How do we accomplish this task? Let's briefly examine the nature of the English language and how meaning is triggered. English is a dynamic, verb-driven language; meaning is signaled by the subject/verb/direct object/indirect object tie. The tighter and stronger the relationship between these elements, the clearer the meaning. The more "noise" or "deadwood" (words that carry little or no meaning) separating these elements, the greater the chances for misinterpretation and breakdown in information flow.

- *Verbs:* Of these elements, the most important is the verb because it tells what happens or what is. The best verbs are strong action words in the simplest form and in the active, not passive, voice. Business writing must move and motivate. It must provide action and energy, not dry, lifeless statements. Prefer "we recommend" (active) to "it was recommended by us" (passive). Write "We exceeded the production quota by 22 percent" (active), not "The production quota was exceeded by 22 percent" (passive).

- *Nouns:* Choose nouns carefully. Prefer simple, specific, concrete nouns; avoid abstract, collective, and category nouns. Remember that the goal of business writing in the United States is to transmit information for decision and action. Action is possible only if meaning is clear. It is easier for readers to visualize and agree on the meaning of "report" than "communication," of a "bill of lading" or "letter of credit" than "documentation." Simple, specific, concrete nouns are clear, vivid, and powerful.

- *Sentences:* Avoid long sentences; they confuse and bore most American business readers. Most sentences become long after about 20 words. Keep the relationship between the subject/verb/direct object/indirect object tight. Think of this relationship as a rubber band and remember that intervening noise will make the band snap.

- *Paragraphs:* Most American business readers hate long, dense paragraphs. Long paragraphs (more than 150 words, or longer than 7–8 typewritten lines) discourage readers. As Strunk and

White state in their classic and much quoted *Elements of Style,* "enormous blocks of print look formidable to a reader." In addition, always use American conventions between paragraphs: either (1) indent the first line five spaces, or (2) double-space between paragraphs.

- *Tone:* Because the underlying philosophy of American business is positive, make sure your tone is courteous, constructive, logical, and persuasive. And because Americans view themselves as energetic and accountable for their actions and decisions, always prefer the active voice in your sentences.

4. Eliminating errors

To be taken seriously by American readers, your document must be professional. Professionalism dictates that you review your writing to eliminate errors by editing, proofreading, and avoiding common mistakes. (See pages 101–109 for details on grammar and punctuation.)

Editing: Editing comprises reviewing your writing for logic, effectiveness, and powerful expression. Break editing into a two-step process:

- *Macro-edit:* Review structure and logic before you revise sentences and refine vocabulary. Edit the "big picture" before you edit the detail, the document and its sections before sentences, and the structure and arguments before the words.

- *Micro-edit:* Evaluate sentences and vocabulary by focusing on your audience. Consider your readers, their requirements, their ease of reading, and their problems understanding and following your analysis and recommendations. Evaluate paragraph and sentence length, accessibility of vocabulary, and general tone from your readers' perspective. Check verbs for power and nouns for simplicity. Eliminate jargon and unnecessary words.

Proofreading: Proofreading consists of examining your writing carefully to eliminate spelling and typographical errors; these mistakes can damage the credibility of your documents. Proofreading is difficult because of the writer's tendency not to see his or her own mistakes. To limit this tendency, consider using several methods simultaneously—use available computer tools (spell check and grammar check software), print out your document to review it (mistakes are often easier to spot on a hard copy than on the computer screen), and ask a colleague to proofread your document for you.

Common mistakes: Be aware of other common mistakes we make when proofreading. Verify the spelling of personal names, titles, company names, and addresses in documents and on envelopes and mailing labels. Double-check the way you handle dates (use month/day/year in the United States), that numbers you use throughout the document add up, and that your use of technical vocabulary and acronyms is in line with corporate policy.

5. Using common business formats

Now that we've discussed the needs of U.S. business readers and the characteristics of effective business writing, let's examine the common business formats you will use during your career in the United States: email, letters, memos, minutes and meeting reports, and executive summaries and briefings. (See pages 95–100 for examples of these common business formats.)

Email: Speed and ease have made electronic mail, or email, pervasive in business today: billions of messages are sent annually. Despite its informality, email is a legally binding business document. When writing email, respect the rules that govern effective writing at your company and remember to:

- *Write a specific, descriptive subject line.* Because American business readers often use the subject line to determine whether to read the message, email messages must have carefully prepared, specific subject lines. Use a specific subject line, such as "Increases in travel budgets effective January 2005" instead of a vague one, such as "Budget issues."

- *Organize your message tightly.* Most screens are limited to 24 or fewer lines. Organize your email message so that related contents can be viewed on one screen; American readers do not like scrolling through multiple screens to find the information they need.

- *Place the important information first.* Even though most readers can glance through several pages of printed matter quickly, they experience difficulty looking at several screens. Use a preview opening to let the reader know total content and make sure your main idea is positioned on the first screen. Remember, many email readers read only the beginning of a message.

- *Use visual layout for readability.* Should your message require several screens, use lists, bullets, headings, and subheadings to assist readers to scroll.

- *Limit attachments.* If your email alludes to a section in another report, attach only that section. If you send the entire report, chances are that it may never be read.

- *Avoid using email for sensitive information.* Remember, your company owns your email. Your boss has the legal right to read your email, even if you have deleted it. In fact, deleted email can almost always be retrieved long after the fact and may even be subpoenaed as legal evidence. So save confidential or problematic information, personal messages, jokes, or disparaging remarks for another medium.

- *Don't "flame"* or write email while angry. Don't be in a hurry to respond, especially if the issue is sensitive or you're irritated. By all means, write the message if it will make you feel better, but let it sit for a while before sending it. Calm down first, then review.

- *Be professional.* Don't irritate readers by shouting (USING ALL CAPS), whispering (writing only in lower case), or forgetting to check spelling and punctuation. Carefully edit and proofread. Don't let the speed or informality of email become a substitute for professional standards or attention to detail.

Letters: The basic format of the modern American business letter provides a definite structure including a heading (identifying where the letter came from), a date line (telling when the letter was written), an inside address (providing name and address of the person to whom you're writing), a salutation (Dear Mr., Dear Ms., Dear Dr.), an opening paragraph (building goodwill and specifying purpose), middle paragraphs (presenting the discussion in short easy-to-read paragraphs), a closing paragraph (wrapping up the discussion, pointing the way to the next step, and building further goodwill), a complimentary close (Very truly yours, Sincerely yours), the writer's name and title (typed), and the signature. (See page 100 for an example letter.) Letters exceeding one page in length should incorporate visual layout (as explained on pages 39–40).

Memos: The memorandum and the multipage memo-report have a standardized format in the United States. Different organizations and corporations dictate their own specific dimensions and design particulars. Memos should have visual layout for immediate readability—listings, headings, graphics—and include the following elements:

- *A descriptive subject line:* To capture your reader's attention immediately, make your subject line as specific as possible within a 10-word limit. Remember, many readers decide whether to read the memo based on the subject line.

- *A strategic opening sentence:* Because your first sentence receives the greatest reader attention (after your subject line), use it to state your purpose, introduce your request, key idea, or question.

- *A closing that identifies the next step:* Write a closing paragraph that is tailored to the purpose of the memo. A good closing emphasizes a key point and motivates your reader to action.

Procedures: A procedure is an explicit work guide that lists chronologically the agents and steps needed to accomplish a task. Procedures break down a task into its component steps and give each step a number to ensure sequential order. Procedure formats range from job guides for individual employees to detailed and complex manuals.

In a simple job guide the same agent performs all the steps. These steps are numbered to reflect order of performance. In complex procedures, the task passes from one agent to another. The best way to show this flow is in a frame that lists the agents in one column and the sequence of steps in an adjacent column.

Minutes and meeting reports: Minutes and meeting reports share and preserve information about problems and projects discussed at meetings. For immediate readability and retrieval of information:

- *Provide a preview:* Write a clear, descriptive subject line, an opening paragraph that summarizes total report content, a list of topics discussed, and an action plan for follow up.

- *Use visual layout:* Make information available "at a glance"; if data are buried in heavy paragraphs, they will be extremely difficult to retrieve.

Executive summaries and briefings: Because executive summaries and briefings are generally prepared for senior management, readability "at a glance" is imperative. Make it easy for your reader to access and retrieve information by organizing it into categories and giving each category a descriptive heading. Be especially careful to use subheadings, listings, charts, and graphs, and to break your content into small paragraphs, short simple sentences, and powerful verbs.

A good executive summary is a stand-alone piece. It can only be written after the report is generated because it requires that you extract the core ideas of your report:

- *Reduce each section of the report.* Extract the key ideas or major arguments by reviewing each section and condensing it into the shortest possible form.

- *Include major items of information.* Because the executive summary must stand alone, remember to summarize the most important facts, figures, analyses, conclusions, and recommendations.

- *Write concisely.* Your goal is to cut the report to a fraction of its original length. The executive summary should be as compact as possible (no greater than one-tenth of the total report).

WRITING GUIDELINES
FOR INTERNATIONALS

To write effectively for American business readers, remember to:

- Address your reader's needs.

- Plan your document: create an outline and choose a logical pattern with your reader in mind.

- Make your writing reader friendly: use descriptive subject lines, complete purpose openings, and thoughtful visual layout.

- Employ an accessible and dynamic style: prefer strong active verbs and simple concrete nouns; avoid long sentences and paragraphs.

- Maintain a positive and persuasive tone.

- Quote or paraphrase information obtained from outside sources.

- Edit and proofread to insure professionalism and eliminate errors.

- Review the essential components of email, letters, memos, procedures, minutes, meeting reports, executive briefings, and summaries.

- Select the appropriate business format to meet your communication goal, and consider your reader when making your choice.

CHAPTER 5 OUTLINE

1. Facing the challenges
2. Developing your message
3. Preparing effective visuals
4. Delivering your message
5. Presentation guidelines for internationals

CHAPTER 5

Powerful Presentations

He who speaks well is at home anywhere.
—DUTCH PROVERB

As we have said throughout this book, Americans value people who communicate directly and well. For example, in Chapter 1 the discussion of individualism focused on the high value Americans place on people who can speak well. From preschoolers participating in "show and tell" activities, high school and college students defending their opinions in debates, and young Americans competing with each other for management slots, to top executives mobilizing their work forces for action, all of U.S. society seems to prize the communicator who can deliver a powerful presentation.

But what is a powerful presentation? And how can you master this skill? Before discussing what makes a presentation interesting and captivating for an American audience, let's examine some facts about communication delivered orally. This information will provide a solid framework for our discussion on developing and delivering presentation content.

I. Facing the challenges

Here are some facts that shed light on the difficulties and challenges that successful and powerful presentations must overcome. Understanding these constraints can help you build a successful presentation.

Retention:

- *The problem:* American audiences retain less than 25 percent of information they hear. Unlike Japanese and Chinese audiences who show a retention level of 90 percent, many American audiences have poor listening skills.

- *The solution:* To counter this deficiency, you need to repeat anything important. You can paraphrase or even repeat verbatim and sound perfectly normal (a technique unacceptable in writing).

Concentration:

- *The problem:* People can think much faster than you can talk. When you are delivering a speech or a presentation, you are competing with the thoughts in your listeners' heads. Your audience may be distracted from what you have to say by weekend plans, analyses of family quarrels, financial concerns, even thoughts about lunch!

- *The solution:* Build rapport by tailoring your message to your audience, telling them why your content is important, or how it will benefit them. Minimize distractions for your American audiences by using simple, punchy, memorable language— active verbs and lively nouns—arranged in short, direct sentences. Long complicated sentences may work for reading but are soporific for listening. As Dorothy Sarnoff, speaking guru to CEOs and politicians says, "The mind cannot accept what the seat cannot endure."

Difficulty of the medium:

- *The problem:* Oral communication is difficult to follow. Your listeners must understand and process information as you say it—at your rate and rhythm of delivery (which may not be theirs). There is no "instant replay" button they can hit.

- *The solution:* State clearly, at the beginning, what your subject is and what structure you will use to discuss it. As you move from one point to another, tell your audience what you are doing. If the subject is complex, stop periodically, remind the audience what you've covered and how much more there is.

Visualization:

- *The problem:* Most human beings think in pictures, not words. Virtually every culture in the world has a proverb that suggests that "a picture is worth a thousand words."

- *The solution:* Illustrate what you have to say with concrete examples or images. For example, don't say that the red ant can carry 20 times its weight for several yards at a time; instead say it is equivalent to a man carrying a Rolls Royce on his back from Paris to Berlin.

2. Developing your message

Now that we've briefly covered some of the constraints of oral communication, let's talk about actually putting together a presentation for an American audience. The steps you need to follow are given here.

Decide what to say.   Define your goals in addressing your audience. Make them specific: the more precisely you formulate your objectives, the more focused and productive your presentation will be. Keep total content short. According to research, most people can understand and remember a maximum of five to seven main points.

Open powerfully.   Open by capturing attention, setting mood, and gaining credibility. Keep your audience in the picture: tell them why the subject should be of interest or of help to them. If you're confused about how to begin, consider the following classic openers:

- *Announce your subject and launch* right into your presentation. Although considered abrupt by many cultures, this direct approach suggests your eagerness to tackle your topic. This opening strikes exactly the right tone for a work meeting or strategy session.

- *Open by referring to the occasion* that brought the audience together. A presentation prepared for a special event or ceremony benefits from this opening.

- *Ask a rhetorical question.* Begin by asking a question or a series of questions to which your listeners know the answer and that will start the audience thinking about your topic.

- *Begin with a startling statement.* This opening is especially effective with a bored or an apathetic audience.

- *Use a quotation.* Choose and open with a quotation to catch the attention of your audience.

- *Begin with an anecdote.* Be sure that the anecdote emphasizes the central point of your talk. If humorous, make certain that the anecdote relates to the specific topic or occasion, will not offend any audience member, and is easy for you to tell.

Put your content in order.   Plan how you will tell your story. Planning allows you to deliver a logical, clear presentation and to control excessive nervousness.

To help you plan, ask yourself the following questions: Who are my listeners? How much do they know about my subject? How can my presentation help them? What do I want my audience to know or do at the end of my presentation? How should I arrange the material to interest or convince my audience? What facts, statistics, comparisons, examples should I use?

If you're unsure about how to order your ideas for coherence and impact, review the common organizational patterns and select the one that works best with the content and the circumstances of your presentation. Some of your choices include:

- *Time sequence:* A chronological pattern (Example: the history of a company or industry)

- *Space sequence:* A locational or geographical pattern (Example: the work flow in an organization)

- *Essential elements:* Important logical divisions of a topic (Example: an economic report on the Middle East divided by country and subdivided into agriculture, mining, and manufacturing)

- *Problem/analysis/solution:* Statement of problem, why it exists, how to solve it or what remains to be done before solution (Example: heavy work loads/ increase in human error/ computer interface)

- *Order of importance:* Ascending or descending importance (Example: universe, continent, country, state, district, county, city)

- *Journalistic sequence:* Who, what, where, when, why and how

- *Pairing:* Grouping correlative ideas such as questions and answers, pros and cons, advantages and disadvantages, causes and effects

Use lively, colorful language.   Research reveals significant differences between communication for reading and for listening. Communication for the ear relies on simple sentences and sentence fragments, rhetorical questions, repetition, contractions, interjections, familiar and monosyllabic words, personal pronouns, active verbs, and concrete nouns.

Many of these differences stem from one simple fact: listeners must understand you as you are speaking; they do not have the luxury of rereading a section or a page. You can help them listen comfortably by using strong verbs, concrete nouns, short sentences, and repetition of key points. You can increase their involvement with your presentation if you paint pictures through vivid words, imagery, and description.

Ineffective example

> Consider two cities, A and B, trading an asset, X. If the prices of X are the same in market A and in market B, then arbitrage may be said to be complete.

Effective example

> Singapore and Malaysia both have markets for junk bonds. The question is, will the bonds sell for the same price in both places?

Close strongly.   Avoid rambling and irritating false endings. Close by summarizing, using a quote, issuing a challenge or appeal. Try to close early rather than late since audiences appreciate a speaker who respects their time.

In addition to the do's suggested, here are two don'ts:

Don't apologize.   Unlike some other cultures, apologizing in the United States violates the unspoken and unwritten contract between audience and speaker—that the speaker is a prepared expert. Apologizing embarrasses American audiences.

Present yourself with full confidence in your experience and knowledge. Concentrate on the information you are trying to share with your listeners, not on any negative feelings you may have about yourself.

Don't read.   Most American presentations are prepared, but not read. Present from index cards or from an outline; if you write out every word, you will end up reading every word. Speeches or presentations that are read tend to irritate American audiences.

- *Prepare presentation notes* by jotting down key concepts, phrases, or words, rather than complete sentences. Many professional speakers use index cards and different ink colors—black for words that relate to content; green for examples, images, or anecdotes; red for instructions about delivery (e.g., "Look at audience" or "Use visual #2"). Number the cards to keep them in the correct sequential order.

- *Prepare manuscript notes* to maximize eye contact. If you have to prepare and deliver a formal, word-for-word presentation, or if you fear total paralysis in the absence of a detailed manuscript, prepare your pages to permit easy reading while maximizing eye contact with your audience. Some pointers to follow:

1. Type in large, bold print. Underline key words you wish to emphasize.

2. Leave one-third of the right side blank for notes. Leave the bottom third blank so you don't drop your head low as you read.

3. Don't break a sentence or paragraph between pages.

4. Don't staple the pages to allow unobtrusive sliding and to minimize distraction to the audience.

5. Number the pages to keep them in order.

3. Preparing effective visuals

Now that we've discussed how you will prepare and structure your content, let's turn our attention to another essential element of American presentations: visual aids.

Although effective visuals take time and thought to prepare, they are well worth the effort:

- *Visuals are memorable:* Nearly 85 percent of the information the human brain receives and retains comes through the eyes. Thus your audience will remember your message much more readily if you use visuals.

- *Visuals communicate difficult data:* Visuals can convey complex ideas and concepts that are difficult to take in through the ears alone. Visuals can clarify financial and statistical data; highlight trends, proportions, and relationships; illustrate economic forecasts, budget comparisons, organization charts, work flow, and many other concepts the audience may find difficult to grasp by merely listening.

To prepare effective visuals, ask yourself "What images do I want to lodge in the minds of my audience?" To do so, follow these basic guidelines:

Keep your visuals simple:

- *Use few words.* Although some words are inevitable in visuals, remember that words are not visual. Avoid creating slides with too many words; use key words and short phrases rather than complete sentences and paragraphs. Don't use your visuals as word-for-word scripts; your audience will not enjoy being read to.

  Instead, let the visual do what words cannot—convey ideas graphically. Words are what you, the presenter, are there for. You provide a unifying element to the words—your audience listens at the speed of your delivery; they read at different speeds.

- *Introduce your visuals clearly.* Use overlays, several visuals, or PowerPoint animation to introduce complex visuals progressively. Visuals that are too complex to be understood at first glance are self-defeating; they frustrate the audience and cause listeners to "tune out."

- *Make your visual large and bold.* Don't force your audience to squint. Use 30–36 point type for titles and 18–24 points for text.

- *Be professional.* Few things are as detrimental to your image as poorly prepared or uncoordinated visuals. Make them neat and use the same font consistently. If possible, test them in the room where you will present.

Choose your colors thoughtfully, not randomly. Be aware of . . .

- *Cultural connotations:* Become familiar with the cultural connotations of color. In the United States, warm colors (reds, oranges, and yellows) connote excitement and dynamism; cool colors (blues, greens, and violets) connote calm and stability; dark colors (black, dark blue, and dark gray) evoke power; red used to show monetary values signifies a negative amount (called being "in the red"); red, white, and blue used together evoke the American flag; and black used alone is associated with death.

- *Background and text:* (1) Background color: Use a cool color (like bright blue) for PowerPoint slides or a light color (like clear) for overheads. (2) Text color: Choose a color that contrasts sharply with your background color (such as bright yellow on bright blue) when displayed on the large screen—not just on your computer monitor.

- *Consistency:* Maintain the same color pattern (for titles and text) throughout your presentation.

- *Not overusing colors:* Do not use too many colors. In general, don't use more than four different colors in any presentation.

- *Physical considerations:* Do not use red and green as contrasting colors because about 8 percent of the population is color-blind.

Select the visual medium with care.   To help you choose, here's a brief discussion of pros, cons, and key points to remember:

- *Computer projections:* Computer software (such as PowerPoint) allows you to produce sophisticated visuals using graphics, color, and animation. A small group (fewer than eight people), can view the visuals directly on your computer screen. In a larger group, you will need to project the images onto a screen.

Because it's so easy to produce interesting visuals with software, there is a tendency to go overboard and clutter your visual with typefaces, clip art, sound, and animation. Remember to keep your visuals simple for best effect.

- *Film and videotape:* Film and videotape are professional, durable, and interesting to the audience. However, they can be expensive to produce and difficult for large audiences to view on a TV monitor. Should you use these media, (1) avoid blasting audience with static: turn on VCR before TV, turn off TV before VCR; (2) be aware of volume level, brightness of room, and other conditions that may affect audience ability to benefit; and (3) consider stopping and starting the film to discuss crucial points.

- *Transparencies:* This durable and flexible visual aid allows highlighting and building information by overlay. If you use transparencies: (1) Keep them simple. Use large type and few words: a maximum of six lines per overhead and six words per line. (2) Present complex information by employing the "reveal" technique (place a piece of paper under transparency and slowly move it down to show one area of information at a time) or overlays (pieces of clear or colored acetate that are taped to the frame and folded back when needed). (3) Use cardboard frames to preserve overhead quality and allow numbering for sequential order.

- *Flipcharts:* Flipcharts are inexpensive, portable, and easy to prepare. However, they do become ragged with use. If you decide to use flips, remember to (1) ensure visibility by making your writing at least 2 inches high; (2) tag flipchart pages for easy reference, or fold the bottom corner of each page for easy turning; (3) use color markers for better visual impact: black or dark blue for text and red or orange for highlighting; and (4) practice to avoid hanging onto flipchart, blocking it from audience view, or turning your back on the audience.

- *Handouts:* Although useful because they spare the audience the necessity of taking notes, they can divert your listeners' attention from you.

Consider making presentations decks (hard copies of your PowerPoint slides) and other handouts available at the end of the presentation.

4. Delivering your message

In the United States, the physical impact of a speaker on the audience is as powerful as anything he or she has to say. To maximize your power as a presenter to American audiences, consider the following points:

Project an effective presence.

- Dress up and take pride in your appearance: doing so is a compliment to your audience.
- Walk briskly to the podium, or to your seat at the conference table. Try to look and feel positive, decisive, and prepared; don't fuss with your person, belongings, or surroundings.
- Use erect posture to project confidence. Lean into the audience and maintain open body language (arms and legs uncrossed and arms open) to suggest openness and interest.
- Use animated gestures. Although gestures may be uncommon in your culture, American audiences prefer animated speakers who gesture to emphasize, mark transitions, or release tension. Relax hands, arms, hips, and knees. Move to release tension preferably at transitional points of speech.
- Maintain eye contact throughout your audience. Business audiences in the United States want you to "look them in the eye"— a mark of honesty and confidence according to their cultural norms.

Project your voice.   Work with your voice to develop power, speed, and clarity.

- Imagine that you are speaking to the last row or back wall to develop correct volume.
- Pause at the end of each sentence for correct speed.
- Enunciate for clarity: make your consonants crisp and your vowels open.
- Vary intonation from loud to soft or move to compensate for lack of variety. Think low to position vocal resonance: deep tones communicate self-assurance and strength.

Don't fear nervousness.   The surge of adrenalin that nervousness causes is nature's way of preparing the body to meet an emergency. It sensitizes you to respond faster, perform better, and concentrate more intensely.

Prefer prepared delivery.   Prepared delivery allows you to be spontaneous in word choice and delivery style yet scrupulously prepared with your content and organization. An unprepared or "impromptu" presentation is never as effective as a prepared presentation; a memorized or word-for-word read speech can come across as wooden and boring.

Prepare to deliver your presentation by developing as much independence as possible from notes. Freedom from notes will increase your authority and improve eye contact, vocal delivery, and spontaneity. If you feel lost without notes, use index cards containing just a few words to jog your memory. If you must use manuscript pages, practice to maximize eye contact and create the illusion of spontaneity.

Prepare and rehearse.   Show your respect for the audience by working on your presentation. Polished presentations that sound spontaneous come from hours of work. Last-minute inspirations rarely lead to memorable speeches. Professionals agree: practice, practice, and practice. (1) Rehearse how you will use your visuals to avoid such common mistakes as searching for a visual while the audience waits, blocking or talking to the visual, or turning your back on your audience. (2) Rehearse your nonverbal delivery, referring to pages 67–79.

Be sensitive to nonverbal messages from the audience.   Even though you're the one talking, your audience is also continually communicating with you nonverbally. Be sensitive to these signals; they can provide valuable clues to alter your presentation. Some common cues include quizzical expressions (they normally signal need for further explanation), restlessness (generally means you should speed up a bit), and audience members looking at their watches (it's time to take a break or finish).

Field questions respectfully.   Always expect questions from an American audience. Instead of fearing questions, welcome them; they signal audience interest and involvement and permit you to show another side of your personality as well as your expertise.

Questions can provide vital information about audience under-standing—as you listen to a question, you can foresee and counter potential problems in understanding. By listening attentively and answering supportively, you can greatly increase your credibility. To manage questions effectively:

- *Listen actively.* Demonstrate your interest and involvement by leaning slightly forward and maintaining eye contact. Your lis-tening skills coupled with genuine interest may even disarm a hostile audience by making them feel understood, supported, and valued.

- *Paraphrase or clarify the question.* To stop possible misinter-pretation and give the audience a feeling of being deeply heard, restate the question in your own words. This repetition will keep you focused on the question and will also buy you some time to think.

- *Support the self-esteem of the questioner* as you answer the question. Never treat a question as stupid. This reaction will polarize your audience and damage your credibility.

- *Admit inability* to answer when that is the case. Do not try to bluff your way out of the situation. Instead, explain how you will obtain the answer later.

- *Move around* when accepting questions so that the total audi-ence feels involved. Keep the pace energetic to prevent the deadly boredom of many question and answer sessions.

- *Resume control* for an appropriate closing. Make sure that you present the last word on the subject.

PRESENTATION GUIDELINES FOR INTERNATIONALS

To deliver effective presentations in American college and business settings, pay attention to the following points:

- Review the challenges that presentations must face to succeed.
- Plan your content and define your goals.
- Open the presentation powerfully: identify the presentation topic and prepare the audience to listen by announcing the agenda.
- Tell your story logically, putting your content in an order that arouses interest and establishes credibility.
- Use lively colorful language based on concrete nouns, strong verbs, short sentences.
- Deliver a powerful closing.
- Prepare effective visuals by applying thoughtful design principles and choosing the appropriate medium.
- Project an effective presence by preparing and rehearsing. Prefer prepared delivery of presentation content.
- Show enthusiasm and sincerity through appropriate eye contact, body language, and gestures.
- Vary intonation patterns, volume, pitch, and resonance in keeping with content.
- Pay attention and respond appropriately to nonverbal messages from the audience.
- Listen carefully and field questions with dignity to listeners and self.

CHAPTER 6 OUTLINE

1. Facial expressions and eye contact
2. Hand gestures and greetings
3. Physical space
4. Other nonverbal behaviors
5. Silence
6. Nonverbal guidelines for internationals

CHAPTER 6

Effective Nonverbal Communication

> Gesture is clearly more than just handwaving—
> it reflects how we think.
> —SUSAN GOLDIN-MEADOW

J ust as culture teaches us about language, we also learn nonverbal
language from our culture at an early age. Our parents and others
teach us how to use our eyes to get and maintain attention, how
to use facial expressions that complement our verbal messages, and
how to use our hands and body to reinforce the impact of our words.
Nonverbal communication conveys meaning without words and
includes eye contact, facial expressions, gestures, and the use of
physical space.

Since experts estimate that 85 percent of communication is nonverbal, learning the English language is only part of your challenge.
Understanding nonverbal cues can be difficult in your own culture; the
problem is magnified if you must translate language and understand
nonverbal cues simultaneously. The assumption that nonverbal communication carries the same meaning no matter what language we
speak may prevent us from interpreting a communication exchange
accurately.

As an international, you may be surprised when you communicate face-to-face with Americans for the first time. The more you
understand and observe the nonverbal elements of communicating in
the United States, the more effective you will be in achieving your
business goals.

1. Facial expressions and eye contact

The international visitor will immediately notice that Americans tend to have animated faces, but the interpretation of various facial expressions may be a mystery to the casual observer from another country. In this section, you will learn the significance of some of the most important facial expressions and eye behavior.

Facial expressions: A challenging aspect of communication for the international businessperson involves the many uses of facial expressions.

- *Smiling:* Americans smile often to indicate friendliness. They may smile at strangers as well as friends.

- *Nodding:* Nodding the head usually indicates that an American is listening and receiving your message. It does not necessarily indicate approval or agreement.

- *Frowning or scowling:* Americans express anger by frowning or scowling.

- *Scowling and smiling:* When eyebrows are squeezed together and the mouth turned upward, the American meaning is usually, "I am confused. What are you talking about?"

- *Raising eyebrows:* This common American expression usually indicates surprise.

- *Squeezing eyebrows together with a frown:* This expression usually indicates doubt as in, "I don't believe that is true."

- *Winking:* Closing one eye has multiple meanings, but the two most common include, "I'm just kidding you" and "I'm flirting with you." It does not indicate a simple greeting as it may in other cultures.

Eye contact: All cultures learn proper eye contact from parents and teachers at an early age as the following example illustrates.

Colleagues at a telecommunications firm in Cincinnati had lunch together at the home of their manager. The manager introduced her two young daughters who played happily while everyone ate. After a pleasant meal and conversation, the children showed everyone their toys, and soon it was time to return to work.

The manager said, "Can you tell our friends thank you for coming to our house?" As she instructed the children, she gently cupped their little faces and lifted them upward. Correctly positioned for appropriate eye contact, the children said thank you and then ran inside the house to their babysitter.

- *Direct eye contact:* In other cultures across the world, and in some subcultures within the United States, direct eye contact is only appropriate between two people of equal rank. In the dominant U.S. business culture, however, direct eye contact is a way of saying, "I respect you as an equal, and I am listening carefully."

- *Indirect eye contact:* In the United States, looking down instead of at the speaker can be interpreted as being insincere, timid, or belligerent. Therefore, we strongly advise that you use direct eye contact in your business communication.

Eye contact and attention: Eye contact can hide problems with communication. For example, Americans are notoriously poor listeners. When businesspeople are tired or distracted, they may look directly at you and even nod as you explain your issues. Do not assume that their direct eye contact and head nodding means that they have heard your message.

After being transferred from Johannesburg to the Seattle office of South Africa Financial, Loan Officer Francis Masekela was pleased that his colleagues increasingly understood him as he mastered the cadences and accents of American English. He was, however, surprised to learn that his direct report, Jim Brown, had not completed several of his requests. After discussing the issue with Jim, Francis realized that he would need to follow his verbal instructions with written ones to ensure that his messages were heard and clearly understood. "Yes, I was fooled by Jim's direct eye contact," he laughed.

Eye contact in American subcultures: During casual conversation, eye contact when speaking and when listening can differ widely among American subcultures.

- *Euro American culture:* When Euro Americans are listening, they tend to gaze directly and constantly at the person who is speaking. When speaking, they may look away from the listener and return their gaze at times to check for direct eye contact that signals listening in their audience.

- *African American culture:* African Americans may use eye contact differently from Euro Americans when speaking and listening. African Americans tend to look directly at the listener when relating a story. They may signal careful listening by looking down or away.

- *Native Americans, Asian Americans, and Latino Americans:* Direct eye contact with elders is a serious breach of etiquette and constitutes a challenge to authority. Children respect elders by casting their eyes downward when listening. Although many have adopted the direct eye contact of the majority culture when communicating at work, some Native Americans may still signal respect for a manager by looking downward.

2. Hand gestures and greetings

Hand gestures can be difficult to understand as the following news item illustrates.

> *During the G-8 meeting in Sea Island, Georgia, in 2004, the careful observer could see many examples of hand gestures and greetings from people around the world. Some who attended made accommodations in their nonverbal communication, but it was difficult to be sure if interpretations were correct.*
>
> *The French are famous for their fine cuisine and temperamental palettes, so reporters asked French President Jacques Chirac to give his opinion of the food at the conference. Chirac gestured to reporters with the thumb and index finger circled. U.S. reporters mistook the hand gesture for the American gesture meaning "OK," everything is satisfactory. However, in France, the thumb and forefinger circle usually indicates "nothing" or "zero."*

American reporters could have asked the French president to clarify his message, but they preferred to interpret his gesture according to their cultural understanding. Internationals who wish to communicate effectively in American business will need to be careful observers and questioners.

Gestures: Most Americans favor large, open gestures. For example, an effective three-minute presentation may involve at least five different gestures plus variations. In an interactive presentation in the United States, you may see the following gestures:

- *Thumb and index finger circle with other fingers extended:* A popular American signal that means everything is going well. The gesture looks a bit like the letters "o" and "k" representing "okay." This gesture has negative or obscene meanings for some other cultures, however, so avoid it when speaking to a multicultural audience.
- *Pointed index finger:* The index finger may be pointed at a member of the audience without indicating rudeness. When presenting to an international audience, however, we recommend using the entire hand with the palm up to indicate a questioner.
- *Palm up in scooping motion*: When beckoning someone, the typical American holds the palm upward and scoops the fingers toward the body. The index finger should never be used to beckon someone as it indicates condescension.

- *Both palms up with shrug:* This gesture indicates that the answer to a question is unknown. It can also suggest confusion.

- *Hands up with palms forward:* This gesture almost universally means, "stop." In American business situations, the gesture is used to calm participants during a contentious debate. Sometimes the hands are waved slightly, and sometimes they are pushed forward as if to physically stop the other person.

- *Thumbs-up* (fist clenched and thumb pointed skyward): The thumbs-up gesture indicates that everything is going well. This gesture has various negative or obscene meanings in other countries, so you would do well to avoid it unless your entire audience is American.

- *Fist pumping:* When an American experiences a victory in sports, he or she may raise a clenched fist and may punctuate it by punching the air. Likewise in business, winning a big contract or making a strong point may elicit the clenched fist gesture.

- *Hand on chin:* When an American places a hand on his or her chin, it usually indicates, "I'm thinking about what you are saying."

- *Crossed arms:* Although someone who crosses arms in front can simply be cold, this gesture many times indicates disbelief or disagreement.

Greetings: U.S. greeting behavior is an extension of the American sense of equality. For example, most Americans greet another person with a face-to-face handshake regardless of differences in rank.

- *Handshake:* Shake hands with an American using your right hand and a firm grip. Leave your left hand at your side unless the person being greeted is a friend. In that case, the left hand can grasp the extended right arm of the receiver of the handshake.

- *Hand wave:* When physical distance is too great for a handshake, the proper greeting in the United States is a hand wave usually with the hand at eye level and facing the other person.

- *Kiss or hug:* At their first meeting, men should refrain from embracing a woman or from kissing her on the cheek, and men should not kiss a woman's hand in greeting. In virtually all business situations in the United States, men do not embrace each other in greeting.

Greetings in American subcultures: The United States includes many subcultures with slightly different modes of greeting.

- *Euro American:* Shake hands and then take one step back or to the side before beginning a conversation.
- *African, Italian, and Latino American:* Greetings may involve touching, hugging, and kissing.
- *Asian American:* A simple nod of the head indicates greeting, and touching may not be appropriate.
- *Native American and Indian American:* Handshake will use less hand pressure.
- *Arab American and Orthodox Jewish:* Arab American men who are practicing Muslims and Orthodox Jews are not supposed to touch a woman in greeting.

3. Physical space

The United States is a large country with low population density, so it is not surprising that people expect to take up a large amount of physical space. Americans tend to favor offices that they do not share; in fact, the size of a person's office and amount of window space can indicate his or her importance to the company. Americans also tend to favor large gestures even though they avoid touching each other when they gesture. In business situations, be aware of the following uses of space.

- *Space while standing:* Most Americans stand about two feet apart when speaking unless they are discussing something private. A man talking to another man tends to stand slightly shoulder-to-shoulder rather than face-to-face because the "face-off" stance can indicate aggression. American women usually face each other as they talk.

- *Space while seated:* In an office conference, many high-ranking American businesspeople will walk from behind their desks and sit in a chair beside you to discuss the matter at hand. At a conference table, the highest-ranking person will sit at the "head" (end) of the table. During a conference, participants will rise and get their own water or coffee as needed.

Posture: A well-educated American businessperson may exhibit slouching posture in informal as well as formal situations. The relaxed posture is a way of saying, "I'm certain of my ideas, and I'm comfortable in my surroundings." An overly erect posture may be interpreted as indicating fearfulness or uncertainty.

- *Leaning forward:* During a discussion, if the listener leans forward, this posture indicates receptiveness or interest in your topic.

- *Leaning back:* During a discussion, if the listener leans away from you, it may indicate a negative attitude toward your message.

Holding hands: American men and women do not hold hands in business situations. Members of the same sex never hold hands in business situations. Hand-holding in the U.S. usually indicates a romantic relationship.

At an economic summit held in the United States, Nigerian President Olusegun Obasanjo grasped and held the hand of the American

President George Bush who reacted with some embarrassment.
Although Mr. Obasanjo was behaving appropriately for his culture
(men holding the hand of other men while walking), his advisors
should have helped him avoid what is considered inappropriate
touching between men in the American business culture.

Likewise, it is unusual for women to hold hands with other women
while walking. American businessmen and women maintain a "privacy bubble" of space around them that should not be violated.

4. Other nonverbal behaviors

If you hope to be successful in the U.S. business culture, you will want to know more than greetings and gestures. Everything about you and the way you behave in business situations will help others form a positive opinion of your preparation and knowledge. In this section, you will learn about appropriate attire as well as nonverbal elements of dinner etiquette.

Dress and accessories: Many cultures use appropriate attire to indicate respect for others in business situations. In an individualistic culture such as the United States where social structures are relatively democratic and personal comfort is valued, the requirements for proper business attire (suit, white shirt, tie for men, and skirted business suit for women) have become less formal. This trend may reverse in the next few years, however. In general, as an international businessperson, you might consider the following suggestions:

- *Avoid attracting attention*: International businesspeople should avoid wearing anything that draws attention. Examples include wild colors and plaids, dangling jewelry, or shiny fabrics.
- *Dress formally when in doubt*: Many situations such as a job interview require traditional business attire. Whenever you are in doubt, wear traditional business attire.
- *Adjust your attire in special circumstances*: You can remove your jacket and tie and roll up your sleeves for a less formal look.

    U.S. Deputy Chief of Protocol, Jeff Eubank wore a business suit and tie to greet the Japanese Prime Minister Junichiro Koizumi during a recent trip to America. When Prime Minister Koizumi emerged from his plane wearing a gray jacket over a plaid shirt with no tie, Mr. Eubank removed his tie and placed it in his pocket.

Dinner etiquette: The opportunity to share a meal together can help any businessperson understand the other culture. As an international businessperson, you will welcome this opportunity as long as you remember a few simple rules for nonverbal behavior.

- *Wait for your guests or hosts*: If you are the first to arrive, and there is no waiting area other than the table, you may be seated. Don't touch anything on the table until everyone is seated, however.

- *Rise when your guests or hosts arrive*: Make sure that you can easily stand when your guests arrive. Extend your right hand as everyone is introduced and maintain eye contact with the person you are meeting.

- *Keep your hands and arms close to your body*: Waving your arms in large gestures is a recipe for disaster because drink glasses can be upturned. Keep gestures small and elbows in.

- *Use utensils for eating, not for gesturing*: Some people can't resist the urge to continue gesturing while holding a fork or knife, but most Americans consider it rude.

- *Keep your mouth shut while chewing*: Always close your mouth when eating. If you take small bites, you can finish chewing and swallowing and still answer questions in a timely fashion.

- *Avoid touching*: Address others by name to get their attention. Never tap them on the shoulder or touch their arm. In addition, dining forces close seating, so observe the physical bubble of space that Americans prefer.

- *Maintain good eye contact*: Restaurants can be noisy, distracting places. Your steady eye contact is the best way to convey your sincere interest in the speaker's conversation.

- *Remove business papers*: Never place business papers on the dining table. Place these under your chair until the end of the meal when plates have been removed.

- *Signal for the bill*: Americans usually signal nonverbally for the check. Raise your index finger while you look toward the server to receive the check.

- *Close the meal*: Place your napkin to the left of your plate and stand up to signal the close of the meal.

5. Silence

Because the American culture values a strict adherence to time schedules, every second of a communication exchange is valuable. Many
consider silence to be a waste of time. Whereas Asian cultures respect
silence as a way of honoring the speaker and considering the message,
the U.S. culture uses silence to indicate a negative response.

> *Amit Patel graduated from a top-ranked university in New Deli
> and accepted a job with an international marketing company in
> their Chicago office. His team researched and planned a formal
> presentation that would be evaluated by a U.S. communication
> consultant. After his team's rehearsal, Amit was pleased to see the
> consultant sitting quietly. No one spoke for several moments.
> Finally, the consultant stated, "I don't know where to begin
> because there are so many problems with your presentation."
> Among other issues, the consultant pointed out that Amit had
> paused too long between his points. "You've got to keep it mov-
> ing, otherwise everyone will fall asleep." Surprised, Amit realized
> that it would take many more months in the American business
> culture before he could properly interpret and use silence.*

Americans interpret silence as indicating one of the following
emotions:

- Unhappiness with your plan or proposal
- Distraction or misunderstanding of your message
- Anger over a situation or a proposed course of action
- Deliberate strategy to encourage a better offer

Therefore, when you observe silence from your American listener,
consider asking careful questions to discover the problem.

NONVERBAL GUIDELINES
FOR INTERNATIONALS

Because nonverbal communication is so important, you will benefit from (1) watching American television, (2) observing and discussing nonverbal communication with friends in the United States, and (3) finding a mentor who will guide you at work.

- *Facial expressions:* Many Americans change facial expressions as rapidly as they speak. Asking speakers to slow down, so that you can better understand them usually slows the pace of the facial expressions as well.

- *Eye contact:* Observe the direct eye contact of successful people in your office environment and adjust your own eye contact as needed. Notice the different use of the eyes when speaking and when listening.

- *Hand gestures:* Never assume that a gesture has the same meaning as it does in your own culture. Until you are sure of the meaning of various gestures and greetings, "keep your hands to yourself."

- *Greetings:* Notice carefully how others in your organization greet each other and then adapt your own greetings to make them more appropriate. Shake hands with the right hand and match the pressure of the other person.

- *Physical space:* Observe the size and placement of offices to understand the relative power of the people in them. Stand still and allow the other party to find a comfortable speaking distance. Maintain an upright but not overly stiff posture. Do not hold hands with or touch others.

- *Other nonverbal behaviors:* Dress similarly to others in your office who have the same job description, and do not wear clothing or accessories that draw undue attention. Be familiar with expectations for dinner etiquette.

- *Silence:* Assume that silence has a negative meaning for your American listener. Avoid long pauses in a conversational exchange or a business presentation.

CHAPTER 7 OUTLINE

1. Understanding American values

2. Establishing your credibility

3. Planning your communication strategy

4. Negotiation guidelines for internationals

CHAPTER 7

Western Negotiation

When it is done well, negotiation is about
solving problems collaboratively.
—DANNY ERTEL
HARVARD NEGOTIATION PROJECT

A recent google.com search resulted in almost *5 million* articles about increased competition in every sector of the U.S. economy: telecommunication, real estate, pharmaceuticals, natural gas, insurance, and many, many more. Excellent negotiating skills have never been more important for success with both native English speakers and those who speak English as a second language.

For the international player, negotiating with a U.S. partner reveals many elements relating to cultural values. This chapter shows what you need to know to be successful when negotiating with Americans:

- Understanding American values
- Establishing your credibility
- Planning your communication strategy

1. Understanding American values

In any culture, underlying values influence every aspect of life. As an international businessperson, you will benefit from understanding how specific American values affect the process of negotiation.

Individual more valued than team: When you negotiate in teams with a U.S. partner, you may notice that every team member is considered equal even though their tasks and responsibilities vary. One person may be identified as the team leader, but this title carries a different connotation than you might expect. The effective U.S. team leader:

- *Conducts brainstorming:* The team leader conducts brainstorming sessions that encourage creative thinking as issues arise during the negotiation.

- *Accepts diverse opinions:* Each team member can speak, and the team leader expects to hear diverse opinions and ideas.

- *Facilitates tasks:* An effective team leader acts as a facilitator by coordinating team members' individual tasks.

Logic more valued than emotion: Western logic usually flows from point A to point B in a straight line. Whereas other cultures may talk "around" a subject, the American negotiator will usually get straight to the main point and the clear reasons that support it. If you take too long to "get to the point," you may not achieve the goals of your negotiation. What might be considered rude in many cultures is simply seen as efficient in the United States. Consider the following aspects of Western logic:

- *Follows a linear line of reasoning:* Americans prefer an abundance of facts and statistical information to support each argument.

- *Avoids emotional appeals:* When a U.S. businessperson refers to another person as "emotional," it is not a compliment.

- *Prefers to start with conclusions:* An executive summary with all conclusions and recommendations may be placed at the beginning of the full written report.

Task more valued than relationships: International negotiators should also understand that Americans tend to do business without necessarily forming long-term relationships with the other party. In fact, Americans distrust relationships to be good negotiating tools and sometimes see them as a disadvantage. "If you are my friend, how can I achieve the best deal?" Dinners and banquets with the U.S. negotiating team are not meant to signal friendship. The very definitions for relationship and friendship may be somewhat different from your native culture:

- *Relationship:* The relationship has a similar meaning to business partnership and is usually temporary and task oriented.
- *Friendship:* The word "friendship" implies friendliness, but not lifelong obligation.

Linear time and profit most valued: As we discussed in Chapter 2, one of the core American values is a linear view of time. When negotiating with a U.S. team, expect Americans to push hard to get things accomplished within tight time frames because they literally believe that "time is money."

> *An experienced salesperson who teaches negotiation skills likes to tell his trainees, "If you agree in haste, you can repent at leisure." He uses this proverb to point to the American tendency to rush through a negotiation. In spite of the trainer's exhortations, he reports that the U.S. trainees have more difficulty mastering patience than any other objective because of the culture's high value of linear time.*

The following are negotiating values that relate to time and profit in the United States.

- *Condensed time frame for profit:* For Americans, three months is a long time, and business profits and losses are measured in quarterly reports. Profit is a prime motivator for Americans, and they must quickly show a profit to succeed. Therefore, U.S. negotiating teams tend to place their profit goals before any other consideration.
- *Bottom-line approach:* Because "Time is of the essence," you may find that U.S. negotiators tend to discuss pricing early in their negotiations. This approach may seem rude to you; however, the American negotiators are simply demonstrating that they give linear time a high cultural value.
- *Work versus life:* You may also observe that because of Americans' short view of time, they may spend extremely long hours

at the office or traveling to achieve their negotiation deadline even when their spouses and children have birthdays or anniversaries. The dates for these birthdays and anniversaries are only celebrated on the actual day when it is does not interfere with business. Otherwise, the day for celebration will be moved to a time that is more convenient.

Written agreements more important than spoken ones: Americans are the most litigious of all societies with the highest per capita ratio of lawyers in the world. If you are a well-informed negotiator, then you will expect that U.S. contracts will be written in a direct and explicit style. In your personal culture, you may be used to judging the personalities and character of the negotiating teams. You will observe, however, that Americans rely on written agreements over intuition or emotion.

- *Letter of transmittal:* A letter of transmittal or cover letter will explain the purpose of the negotiation.
- *Legal contract:* The legal contract will contain only the specifics of the negotiation agreement and will provide space for signatures.

Americans will discount anything that is not agreed to in writing. To a U.S. negotiator, it really doesn't count until "your name is on the dotted line."

2. Establishing your credibility

Communication expert Mary Munter describes five elements that affect credibility in U.S. business: rank, goodwill, expertise, image, and common ground. Although these elements help establish credibility any time you speak to Americans, you will find them especially helpful when you negotiate.

Rank: In U.S. business discussions, middle managers are free to negotiate with upper level managers in another company because a strict hierarchy is not as defined as it is in other cultures. In addition, family and university affiliations are less important to Americans. U.S. negotiators, however, will want to know whether the people they are talking to have decision-making power. "Are we talking to the decision maker?" is often heard when parties prepare to negotiate in the United States. The power to agree to terms and sign a contract, therefore, carries importance that is similar to rank.

Goodwill: Munter defines goodwill as the personal relationship or past experience with the other party. Because relationships are relatively less important in America, and because they tend to be temporary, it's important for the international negotiator to emphasize the other party's material benefits and timing considerations and not rely solely on goodwill.

Expertise: Expertise refers to knowledge and competence. In the American culture—where facts, figures, and exact specifications carry huge importance—expertise credibility carries high value. Therefore, international negotiating teams need to clearly establish past experience and sound technical knowledge. It is common in the United States to provide a list of prior clients and to discuss in some detail their record of success.

Image: Image involves the extent to which the other party finds you attractive and wants to be like you. If you already look and sound similar to your audience, you will automatically have the advantage of image credibility. Image can therefore present a possible impediment to the international negotiator.

- *Variable elements*: Height, gender, ethnicity, and age are all factors of image that cannot be changed; however, English fluency and attire are two examples of things that you can adjust to help establish image credibility.

- *Definitions of success*: Americans like to do business with other successful people. You and your negotiating team should strive to convey the image of success through hard work, however, rather than through family wealth or connections.

  Anita Barton uses her MBA and an MPH (Masters of Public Health) to consult with corporations in formulating their drug and alcohol abuse policies and treatment programs. Because she is an attractive blonde in her early thirties, she sometimes finds it difficult to establish image credibility with potential business clients in the United States. Therefore, Anita is careful to spend time discussing her experience and trying to find common ground through education, work with client organizations, and other evidence of her credibility. Her business has thrived in spite of the "handicaps" of age, gender, and physical appearance.

Common ground: Common ground credibility involves evoking values that you share with your audience. Knowing the following areas of possible common ground will be helpful during your preparation to negotiate in the United States:

- *Shared tangible benefits:* Benefits include profit, savings, bonuses, or product discounts.

- *Career or task benefits:* Career or task benefits include solving problems, saving time, or advancing prestige.

- *Ego benefits:* Ego benefits include self-worth, accomplishment, and achievement.

- *Group benefits:* Group benefits include relationships, group identity, solidarity, or consensus.

3. Planning your communication strategy

Using a strategic approach to business communication may be the single most important element when negotiating in the United States. As a successful international negotiator, you will define your purpose, analyze your audience, focus on time and money issues, be persuasive, practice your presentation, and bring the negotiation to a successful close. First, though, you will need to select your negotiating team.

Select your team carefully. As an international negotiator, you will do well to choose team members with at least several of the following desirable characteristics:

- English fluency and knowledge of vocabulary relating to your negotiation, or ability to work with a translator
- Familiarity with the American culture
- Knowledge of a particular specialty
- Experience in negotiating

To create a team similar to many American negotiating teams, you might select a technical engineer, an accountant, a sales representative, and an administrative assistant with your designated team leader acting as overall facilitator. In U.S. negotiating, each team member is usually responsible for a different part of the presentation and negotiation. The engineer may discuss technical aspects, while the plant manager will discuss process. A quality assurance (QA) representative will cover quality issues, and the sales representative will discuss price. You can design a team that functions in a similar manner.

If your team members do not speak English fluently, simultaneous translations can improve your results with international trading partners.

At a recent trade conference in Mexico City, international parties were able to hear presentations translated as they were spoken. Each participant could hear the translator's voice in an earphone similar to the service utilized at the United Nations. The participants reported that they were much less fatigued and understood more of the material presented at the conference than when translation was sequential. A participant reported, "There was a more natural exchange among the participants. We also had better follow-up after the conference. I think it's a great tool."

Once you've carefully selected your negotiating team, consider the following strategy for communicating effectively.

Set your objectives.   During your first meeting with your negotiating team, spend time clearly defining your purpose and setting your objectives. For example, your objective may be to conduct a joint venture, sell products, provide service, or negotiate a labor contract.

Analyze your U.S. audience.   After defining your purpose for negotiating, your first step as an international negotiator will be to analyze carefully the needs of your audience.

• *Research the company:* Read the company's annual report to know more about its history. Look at current news stories. Examine data from independent financial sources. Talk to people in the company.

• *Analyze priorities:* Ask questions designed to determine the other party's priorities. For example, how do they rank concerns such as price, delivery schedules, product or service quality, packaging specifications, training, warehousing space, shipping details, labor guarantees, governmental oversight issues, ethical assurances, customer service, technology provisions, opportunities to bid on future contracts, and others.

> *The head of sales for a giant telecommunications company located in Phoenix, Arizona, recently stated that the most important element of any negotiation is preparation of his team. "We need to know everything about our potential buyer's business. We read annual reports, interview plant managers, talk to buyers, read news reports, and ask lots of questions. We do this* before *we start the actual sales negotiation."*

Focus on time and money.   Knowing the American negotiating style will help you understand their strategy. The following concerns will be important to them.

• *Time concerns:* A concern for the U.S. team will be on-time delivery or completion of a contract. Be prepared to emphasize your ability as an international company to deliver a product or service within a specific time frame. If you believe that you will need extra time, be prepared to discuss issues relating to possible delays.

- *Price concerns:* A low price may overcome negative time issues, because a good price is usually the primary objective of the U.S. negotiating team.

Plan ahead for concessions. Because American negotiators value time and money above other objectives, you can expect them to offer concessions in those two areas. Your team should similarly plan the range of prices that you believe are acceptable.

- *Offer concessions:* To negotiate successfully with an American team, set a top and bottom price and plan to offer a slight reduction in price several times before you signal your final offer.

- *Ask for concessions:* Each time you give a concession on price or time, ask for a concession from the American team.

   Before emigrating to the United States, Ali Karzah grew up in a Middle Eastern culture where haggling over prices was commonplace. As a manager for a soft drink company, he quickly discovered that most Americans expect to pay a fixed price for goods and services. "I am amazed that in the strongest country in the world, our employees have to learn the give and take of negotiation by attending training courses."

Be persuasive. To be persuasive with the American audience, avoid emotional arguments. American negotiators typically distrust a show of strong emotion and may even assume that an overt display of emotion is manipulative. Statements that you deliver in a professional tone will be more persuasive. Additionally, the following steps will enhance the persuasiveness of your international negotiating team:

- Help the U.S. party to understand there is a problem and offer a solution.
- List the points of agreement to encourage acceptance.
- Offer your proposal in the simplest form—perhaps offering a pilot program first.
- Ask questions to reveal possible objections to your proposal, and then address them.

Practice your presentation: Review the advice in Chapter 5 to enhance your team's presentation skills. Rehearsal should include not only the points to be covered in your presentation, but also your overall communication strategy. With your team, anticipate possible questions from the other negotiating team based on information you have learned about the American culture. Your practice in answering these questions will ensure a more successful negotiating session.

Ask for feedback.   At the end of your negotiation with a U.S. team, you should go over the agreed-upon points step-by-step, modifying them slightly for clarity or to address the concerns of the other party. Ask questions to clarify each point before making your final agreement, because the Americans will expect the contract to be final.

Plan for unresolved issues.   During negotiation, there may be disagreements on several key points in spite of your desire to complete the negotiation. In such a case, a knowledgeable mediator can help you and your negotiating partner reach an agreement. In cases where an agreement has been reached but breaks down, third-party arbitration may be the best choice.

NEGOTIATION GUIDELINES FOR INTERNATIONALS

To negotiate successfully in the U.S., remember to ...

Understand American values and how they affect negotiations.

- Expect U.S. team members to express individual opinions.
- Address your remarks to any person on the U.S. team, not just the team leader.
- Prove your points with facts rather than emotional appeals.
- Expect the Americans to be friendly, but do not expect long-term friendships.
- Emphasize benefits such as linear time and profit.
- Put all agreements in writing.

Establish credibility with U.S. negotiators.

- Deemphasize your hierarchical rank and your family connections.
- Emphasize material benefits to the other party.
- Present facts relating to your personal and company expertise.
- Speak slowly and clearly.
- Emphasize that your company is working hard to ensure success.

Use a strategic approach.

- Select team members carefully.
- Define your goals. What would you like to achieve?
- Analyze the needs of your audience and think of ways to meet those needs as you fulfill your own objectives.
- Focus on time and money issues.
- Practice your presentation with your team members.
- Plan for mediation or arbitration if you have unresolved issues.
- Ask questions frequently to make sure your audience understands your proposal.

PART III

Writing References for ESL

1. Formats for Business Writing
2. Grammar, Usage, and Syntax
3. Punctuation

REFERENCE I

Formats for Business Writing

The most common formats for business communication are email, memos, executive summaries, meeting reports, and letters. This section will provide examples of these important tools for communicating with American readers.

Example of Email Format

The use of email is extremely prevalent in U.S. business. See pages 44–45 for email writing techniques.

Wednesday, September 2, 2004 3:09:35 PM
From: Molly Brighton
Subject: PR Expert Panel on Thursday
To: Communication Team Conference (mmunt@techsyst.com,
    sreyn@techsyst.com, dvale@techsyst.com, ngrav@techsyst.com)

Before the Ogani software debut, we have an exciting opportunity to receive training from some of the country's leading PR practitioners on September 14 at 1:00 in the executive conference room on the 4th floor. This will be an excellent opportunity for you to prepare yourself for the media interviews in October.

At the meeting, you will:

- Receive media kits
- Participate in a video analysis of sample questions
- Meet the PR person responsible for arranging your interviews

See you there.

Molly Brighton
Director, External Communication
Technology Systems, Inc.
1300 Rafferty Road
Albany, NY 20322-2710
412.727.0000 (Reception)
412.605.0001 (Voicemail)
mbright@techsyst.com

Example of Memo Format

American businesses use memos when they communicate with audiences internal to the company or organization. See pages 45–46 for tips on writing memos.

Date: September 2, 2004

From: Molly Brighton

Subject: PR Expert Panel on Thursday

To: Communication Team (Mary Munty, Sam Reynolds, Delores Valentinos, and Nicola Gravinski)

Before the Ogani software debut, we have an exciting opportunity to receive training from some of the country's leading PR practitioners on September 14 at 1:00 in the executive conference room on the 4th floor. This will be an excellent opportunity for you to prepare yourself for the media interviews in October.

At this meeting, you will:

- Receive media kits
- Participate in a video analysis of sample questions
- Meet the PR person responsible for arranging your interviews.

See you there,
Molly

Example of Executive Summary Format

An executive summary or briefing summarizes the main ideas of a longer document, including your conclusions, recommendations, and implementation steps. See pages 46–47 for tips on writing executive summaries.

Internal Audit of Receivables Balance

The purpose of this internal audit is to identify untapped income and areas of loss for Swingmorrow, Inc. We have posted complete data on the company intranet in a password-protected area viewable only by our department heads and directors. Please review the data before the annual meeting on December 7.

We identified three ongoing problems in the second quarter:
- Accounts receivable increased from $3.75 to $3.97 million, making our total receivables more than $4 million.
- Departments are not sending billing statements to customers within 30 days.
- Monthly receivables reports do not specify department. This results in delayed billing when department heads believe other departments have already billed customers.

We recommend the following actions:
- To reduce receivables, all departments will collect on invoices within 90 days.
- To speed collection, we will update customer billing statements within 30 days.
- To reduce confusion within departments about the monthly receivable reports, we will engage a consultant specializing in statement design.

The audit committee will vote on these recommendations at the annual meeting in December.

Example of Meeting Report Format

Minutes and meeting reports share and preserve information about issues discussed at meetings, as explained on page 46.

MEETING REPORT
December 2, 2004

Attending: Calvin McDonough, Budget Director; Alvarez Alavi, Training Coordinator; Maryam DeJarnett, Director of Information Systems

Objective

The purpose of this meeting was to approve the training program for the following Information Systems Division employees: Charles Smith, Simeon Ray, Alexis Hughes, Ravi Shah, and Dee Ibragimova.

Notes

1. Training will be provided by ABS Services of Toronto, Canada. ABS Services is an approved service provider.
2. The IS employees will report to Development Office # 2, from 8:00 a.m. to 4:00 p.m. on Tuesday, June 14, for the training.
3. Training will include data administration and workflow management.
4. The training will cost $225 per person. This amount is within the approved budget.

Action

After discussing the proposed training, the directors approved the budget allocation.

Example of Letter Format

American business writers use letters when they communicate with external clients and customers, as explained on page 45.

A basic format for an American business letter is shown below. However, always check your company to see whether it uses an alternate, preferred style.

Technology Systems, Inc.
1300 Rafferty Road
Albany, NY 20322-2710

September 24, 2005

Ms. Anandi Bhardwaj
Grandview Technology
1141 Industrial Blvd.
San Mateo, CA 94227

Dear Ms. Bhardwaj:

We would like to invite you or your representative to attend an information session on procedures for submitting government contracts. Your attendance will ensure that your proposals meet government standards: you will learn about required formats, quality standards, and pricing restrictions.

Event:	Government contract information session
Date:	Friday, October 22, 2005
Time:	9 a.m. to 5 p.m.
Place:	Technology Systems, Inc.
	Building II, Training Room
	1300 Rafferty Road
	Albany, NY 20322

To ensure that we have enough refreshments, please contact Tom Dashoff to confirm your attendance. Tom's number is 412.727.1222, and his email is tdash@techsyst.com. If you are unfamiliar with our location, Tom will send you an email with a map to our facility.

We look forward to meeting you and providing information that will make your job easier.

Sincerely,

Ali Babar

Ali Babar
Training Director

REFERENCE 2

Grammar, Usage, and Syntax

Using correct grammar, usage, and syntax will enhance your credibility. Reference 2 explains these important issues.

Agreement (pronoun/antecedent):

Your pronoun should agree with its antecedent.

- *Use a singular pronoun:* Use singular pronouns to refer to antecedents such as person, woman, man, kind, each, either, neither, another, anyone, somebody, one, everybody, and no one.

  Each woman on the committee should submit **her** travel voucher to the accountant.

- *Use the closer noun:* Use the noun that is closest to the verb to determine the pronoun for subjects joined by *or* or *nor*.

  Neither Anjay nor Kimi has completed **his** (not *their*) report.

- *Use a singular pronoun:* When the noun is collective, use the singular pronoun.

  The group is preparing **its** (not *their*) report.

Agreement (subject/verb):

The subject and verb should agree in number.

- *Subject location:* Make sure that you locate the subject and verb in each sentence. If the subject is singular, use a singular verb. If the subject is plural, use a plural verb. Both of the following examples are correct.

  The **risks** of takeover **seem** great. (*risks* is the subject and *seem* is the verb)

  The **risk** of takeover **seems** great. (*risk* is the subject and *seems* is the verb)

- *Subjects linked by conjunctions:* Use the number of the noun closest to the verb when the subject is linked by *or* or *nor*, either . . . or, and neither . . . nor:

  Either the board members or the secretary **has** (not *have*) the key.

- *Subject-verb agreement with collective nouns:* Use a singular verb for collective nouns such as group, family, committee.

  The committee **has** (not *have*) a meeting today.

- *Special subjects:* Use a singular verb for subjects such as each, either, another, anyone, someone, something, one, everybody, no one, and nothing.

  Another **one** of the members **has** (not *have*) the invoice.

Articles and noun determiners:

The three articles (*a, an, the*) point to nouns within the sentence, so they are sometimes referred to as "noun determiners." Some internationals have difficulty knowing when to use articles because their native language may not use articles in the same way as American English. Others may have learned British English where the use of articles is somewhat different.

- *Indefinite articles: A* and *an* are indefinite articles because they do not specify a particular noun. Use *a* before consonants or consonant sounds. Use *an* before vowels or vowel sounds.

  Parking is **an** issue that we would like to discuss (implies that parking is one issue that will be discussed).

- *Definite articles: The* is a definite article because it points to a specific noun.

  Parking is **the** issue we would like to discuss (implies that parking is the only issue that will be discussed).

- *Articles before abbreviations:* Select an article based on the initial sound of the abbreviation whether it is pronounced as a word or as initials.

  A NATO representative asked for information on shipment of supplies.

  An MBA degree would help anyone who wants a promotion in this company.

Numbers:

Here are some important conventions to remember when writing numbers for an American audience.

- *Spell out small numbers:* Standard usage usually recommends that you spell out the numbers from one to ten and use Arabic numerals for numbers higher than ten.

   We achieved our goal of **ten** new accounts during the month of October. In November, we exceeded our goal and signed **15** new accounts.

- *Be consistent:* When you want to emphasize the number, you can use Arabic numerals for numbers from one to ten. However, if you break this rule, be consistent throughout your document.

   We opened **10** new accounts in October when our goal was only **5**.

- *Spell out sentence-starters:* To improve the readability of your document, always spell out a number that starts a sentence even if the number is greater than ten.

   Twenty-eight sales associates attended the weekly meeting.

- *Use Arabic numerals:* Use Arabic numerals to express decimals, percentages, dates, dollar amounts, and the time of day.

   On May **20**, by **5:00** p.m., about **8** percent of our online hits resulted in a sale.

- *Note the time correctly:* In the United States, business communicators use the 12-hour format (a.m. and p.m.) to express time. (Only the airlines, the military, and emergency personnel use 24-hour time expressions such as 1300 hours.)

   We invited the speakers to a reception at **6:00 p.m.**

   You may also see many business writers omitting the periods.

   The business speaker's brunch will begin at **11:00 am** and will be followed by a tour of the new building.

- *Use American style to write the date:* The U.S. convention for writing the date differs from many international formats. Almost every country in the world except the United States writes the day before the month: 22 September 2003 or 22/9/03. In the U.S., however, write the month first: October 22, 2006 or 10/22/06. To avoid confusion, always spell out the month followed by the day and the year.

- *Use telephone numbers correctly:* (1) *Writing phone numbers:*
  In the United States, phone numbers include a three-digit area
  code and a seven-digit phone number. Write a U.S. phone number with spaces, with periods, or with dashes as the following
  three examples illustrate:

  234 555 1234

  234.555.1234

  234-555-1234

  (2) *Dialing within the United States:* To call a local number,
  dial the seven-digit number only. To call long distance to a different area code, dial 1, then the three-digit area code and
  seven-digit number. (3) *Dialing outside the United States:* To call
  from the United States to an international number, dial an international access code (such as 011 or other numbers, depending on
  your service provider), then the country code, city code, and local
  number. *Note:* Most Americans are unfamiliar with the symbols of
  the plus sign, a country code, or a city code, because these symbols are not used in the United States. Therefore, most of them
  would probably not understand what this notation means: +48-22-
  504-2345.

Sentence syntax and voice:
As we explained on page 41, the English language is driven by verbs.
Most of the sentences in your business document should consist of a
subject, action verb, and object (SVO). The SVO arrangement will
help you write English sentences in active voice.

- *Prefer the active voice with SVO:* In the following example, the
  subject is *firm*; the verb is *created*: and the object is *report*.

  The marketing **firm** of Watson & Hemenez **created** our
  annual **report**.

- *Avoid the passive voice:* In the following example, the *report*
  becomes the subject, the verb becomes *was created* and there is
  no object. The sentence needs the prepositional phrase *by Watson
  and Hermenez* to give complete information to the reader.

  Our annual **report was created by** Watson and Hemenez, a
  local marketing firm.

REFERENCE 3

Punctuation

Try to be especially careful to use the following punctuation marks correctly. Correct punctuation marks guide your reader to the proper interpretation of your written business communication. Whenever in doubt about punctuation, consult a handbook with a current copyright.

Apostrophe:

- *For singular or plural nouns **not** ending in s or z:* Add the apostrophe and *s*.

   McCloskey**'s** account; worker**'s** rights; one**'s** own

   Mr. Gonzalez requested that the dealer honor the car**'s** warranty.

- *For singular nouns ending in an s or z sound:* Add the apostrophe and *s*.

   My boss**'s** office is down the hall.

- *For plural nouns ending in an s or z sound:* Add only the apostrophe.

   The Brogdons**'** account was established in 2004.

   He purchased several million dollars**'** worth of liability insurance for the business.

- *Individual and group possession:* Use the apostrophe to differentiate between individual and group possession.

   Gupta and Hall**'s** account will be closed at the end of the fiscal year (joint ownership).

   Gupta**'s** and Hall**'s** accounts will be closed next month (individual ownership).

- *Omission of letters in contraction:* Use the apostrophe to indicate where a letter is missing in a contraction.

   They're (they are) planning to attend the meeting in June **'05** (2005).

- *Abbreviations:* Use an apostrophe and *s* to form the plural of lowercase letters. When needed to avoid confusion, use the apostrophe and *s* to form the plural of capital letters and abbreviations not followed by periods.

  The exacting manager crosses his **t's** and dots his **i's**.

- *Do not use apostrophe:* The apostrophe is unnecessary with the pronouns *his, its, ours, yours, theirs*, and *whose*, with plural nouns that do not show possession, or with plural acronyms.

  His department contributed the financial data; **ours** (not *our's*) provided the artwork for marketing.

- *Writing tip:* Do not confuse *its* with *it's* or *whose* with *who's*.

  It's (*it is*) no wonder the company is unable to locate the information; **its** filing system is antiquated.

  She's an accountant **whose** results are reliable.

  She is an accountant **who's** (*who is*) reliable.

Comma:

- *Separate items in a series:* Use a comma to separate items in a parallel series of words, phrases, or subordinate clauses. Unlike British usage, American usage prefers a comma before *and*.

  Their assistant distributed pens, pencils, calendars, and handouts to the participants.

- *Separate independent clauses:* Use a comma to separate independent clauses joined by the coordinating conjunctions *and, or, nor, but, yet, so, for*. Remember that an independent clause will contain both a subject and a verb as shown in italics in the following sentence.

  She presented her information to the department, and *she answered* many questions about the data

- *Set off introductory elements:* Use a comma to set off most introductory elements. In addition, use a comma after introductory transition words such as *for example, however, finally*.

  If you find that you have a fairly long introductory element at the beginning of your sentence, use a comma before your independent clause.

- *Set off incidental information:* Use commas to set off phrases or clauses within the sentence that interrupt the flow of the sentence and that are not essential elements for the under-standing of the sentence.

The board, having interviewed candidates for three months, found a replacement for the CEO.

- *Punctuate dates:* When writing dates in a sentence, use a comma before and after the year.

The board of directors met on March 2, 2006, with 200 share-holders in attendance.

- *Separate double adjectives:* Use a comma to separate two adjectives that modify the same noun.

The long, detailed report revealed many examples of negligence

- *Avoid commas between two sentences:* Do not use a comma between two sentences. This error is called a "comma splice," because you mistakenly use a comma to connect (or "splice") two independent clauses without using a coordinating conjunction. Three methods correct a comma splice: add a coordinating conjunction such as *and,* use a semicolon, or rewrite the sentence as two sentences.

Incorrect comma splice: She presented her information to the department, she answered many questions about the data.

Corrected examples: She presented her information to the department, **and** she answered questions about the data. *OR* She presented her information to the department; she answered questions about the data. *OR* She presented her information to the department. Then, she answered questions about the data.

Colons:

- *Introduce a list:* The colon follows a noun to introduce a list, a quotation, a clause, or a word.

We represented the interests of the following constituencies: shareholders, management, and employees.

- *Business letter greeting:* Use a colon after the salutation of a typed, formal business letter. (If you handwrite a more informal letter, you may use a comma instead.)

Dear Ms. Starkhov:

Dash:

- *As a strong comma:* Use the dash where you would use a comma when you want a stronger summary or a more emphatic break. Use a dash to emphasize interruptions, informal breaks in thought, or parenthetical remarks—especially if they are strong or contain internal commas.

  Use the dash for a stronger—more emphatic—break.

- *Do not use:* Avoid using the dash in place of a period or in place of a semicolon between two independent clauses.

- *Type a dash:* Type a dash—with no space before or after the surrounding words—as two hyphens. Most word processing programs will automatically convert the two hyphens to a dash, or you can use "option/shift/hyphen."

- *Writing tip:* When in doubt, avoid using the dash in business writing.

Exclamation point:

- *Strong feeling:* Exclamation points show strong feeling.

  Congratulations! You are the employee of the month.

- *Writing tip:* Avoid exclamation points in most business writing and avoid them entirely in formal business reports.

Hyphens:

- *Compound adjectives:* Use a hyphen between multiple adjectives to distinguish between the modifier and the noun.

  We purchased a **high-speed** computer

  She became adept at **cut-and-paste** editing

- *Numbers greater than twenty:* Use a hyphen when you write out numbers from **twenty-one** to **ninety-nine**.

- *Hyphen with "self" followed by a noun:* Use a hyphen after *self-* when it is followed by a noun as in *self-disclosure*

  Sanitare, Inc. takes pride in the ethics of **self-disclosure**.

- *After ex-:* Use a hyphen after *ex-* as in **ex-employee**.

Period:

- *End of declarative sentence:* Use a period to signal a full stop to your reader.

  The board held its regular annual meeting on July 25.

- *Abbreviations:* Indicate the shortened form of a word with a period. Avoid abbreviations in formal business documents.

  They will ship the package on **Fri.** of next week.

- *Writing tip:* Explain abbreviations and acronyms clearly the first time you use them in a business document. Avoid using acronyms such as ASAP (as soon as possible) unless you are certain the receiver will understand your meaning.

  The **GSP (Grummond Strategic Plan)** explains all steps involved in planning requirements.

Question mark:

- *Direct question:* Indicate a direct question with a question mark.

  Why do we leave the office lights on at night?

- *Indirect question:* Indicate an indirect question with a period, not a question mark.

  He asked what report I was writing.

Quotation marks:

- *Indicate a title:* Use quotation marks to indicate titles of short articles within a larger work. Use italics to indicate the longer work.

  Example: He read "KO's Knockout Punch" in the *Wall Street Journal.*

- *Indicate a quote:* Quotation marks set off words that indicate a direct statement. If you use only part of a statement, place commas around only the quoted material.

  The division manager said, "The only thing we have to fear is bad third quarter profits."

- *Punctuate correctly around quotation marks:* As in the preceding example, always place commas and periods *within* the quotation marks, but place the colon and semicolon *outside* the quotation marks.

- *Writing tip:* Use quotation marks to avoid plagiarism. The quotation marks indicate that you have used the exact words from a book or article. In addition to quotation marks, include the source of the quoted material, so that others can refer to the original source. Because many email programs convert quotation marks to symbols upon transmission, clearly identify quoted material that you send via email (as illustrated here).

  The following paragraph contains the exact wording about the merger from the 2005 annual report.

Semicolons:

- *Separate items in a list:* If your list already includes commas, use the semicolon to separate the elements.

  We met in past years on the following dates: July 20, 2003; July 22, 2004; and July 12, 2005.

- *Separate independent clauses:* When the second clause is introduced by a conjunctive adverb such as *however, therefore, nevertheless, furthermore*, or *consequently*, place a semicolon before the conjunctive adverb.

  Our accounting department reported a correction for the January profit statement; however, we will not correct the error until the February report.

- *Separate independent clauses:* Use a semicolon between closely related independent clauses.

  The part we ordered has arrived; it had been on back-order since June 11.

PART IV

Resources for ESL

A: Questionnaire for Self-
Understanding

B: Online Resources

C: Bibliography

D: Novels About the U.S. Culture

E: Films About the U.S. Culture

RESOURCE A

Questionnaire for Self-Understanding

One important tool for the international businessperson is cultural understanding. We designed the following questionnaire to help you understand your own cultural tendencies and see similarities and differences between your native culture and the American culture. For each of the following numbered items, select the answer that more closely approximates your beliefs and behavior.

Chapter 1: American Individualism

1. Your group has been assigned a new project. What is your feeling about it?

   (A) You would rather do it on your own and finish faster.

   (B) You look forward to learning more by working with the team.

2. The division in your company that has the most sales for the third quarter will win a 10 percent bonus. The highest salesperson in the overall company will earn an additional 20 percent bonus. How would you approach the contest?

   (A) Double your efforts to win the 20 percent individual bonus.

   (B) Meet with your group to devise a plan to ensure that your division wins.

3. You are taking a train or entering a restaurant. Neither the train car nor the restaurant is full. Which of the following options would you choose?

   (A) You select a seat away from other people.

   (B) You select a seat near other people.

4. Your company is expanding to South America and you have been sent to meet with the Venezuelan representative. How do you approach the meeting?

   (A) You fly to Caracas, plan to meet and return the following day.

   (B) You fly to Caracas a day early to tour, so that you can comment on the beauty of the countryside and the history of the nation when you meet with the representative.

5. Your meetings with the international team have lasted all day. What do you do after hours?

   (A) Make your excuses and retire for the night.

   (B) Believe it is your obligation to go out with the group no matter how tired you are.

   Calculate your score. If you chose more A answers, your attitudes align more closely with an individualistic culture. More B answers may indicate that you align with a more collective culture.

Chapter 2: American Attitudes Toward Time

6. You are on vacation. The mass transit train arrives late and the platform is quite crowded. What do you do?

   (A) Push forward.

   (B) Wait patiently to board.

7. At the office, you are on the phone when you see a colleague walk toward you. Because he's been traveling, you haven't seen him in a month. What do you do?

   (A) Smile and wave and hold up your finger to indicate, "Wait a minute."

   (B) Terminate the call, so you can greet your colleague.

8. Do you carry a PDA, day planner, or calendar with appointments?

   (A) Yes

   (B) No

9. Are you comfortable doing multiple tasks at the same time?

   (A) No

   (B) Yes

10. Are your business colleagues and the group you socialize with usually similar?

   (A) No

   (B) Yes

   Calculate your score. If you chose more A answers, you may tend toward a linear time orientation. If you scored more B answers, you may be from a flexible or cyclical time orientation.

Chapter 3: American Business Relationships

11. You've worked with the new vice president for several months and have formed an opinion of her. You like her for the following reason.

   (A) She listens to various opinions and seeks consensus.

   (B) She takes charge and doesn't allow arguments.

12. You have been selected by the head of your department to be a team member on a big project. At the first team meeting, some people suggest that the team select a leader.

   (A) You disagree. No one should be singled out as higher in rank than the others.

   (B) You agree. The team will accomplish more with clear leadership and structure.

13. Your division is facing cutbacks, and you must decide how they should be accomplished. What would you do?

   (A) Call a meeting of employees to discuss options.

   (B) Cut everyone's salary 3 percent.

14. You've been introduced to economist Dr. Rodrigo Barbato from a prominent university in Madrid. You address him in the following manner:

   (A) It's nice to meet you, Rodrigo.

   (B) It's nice to meet you, Dr. Barbato.

15. You will be meeting with representatives of a South Korean electronics firm. You decide to wear the following:

   (A) Business casual attire

   (B) Business attire

   Calculate your score. If you chose more A answers, you may tend toward a more democratic view of business relationships. If you scored more B answers, you probably have a more hierarchical view of business relationships.

RESOURCE B
Online Resources

The following links lead to helpful sites specifically designed to assist businesspeople who speak English as a second language (ESL) communicate more effectively. Explore these sites to find the ones that will be most useful and specific to your needs. Please note, however, that we are not endorsing these products or services.

1. *Dave's ESL Café:* Dave's ESL Café offers a menu of resources for internationals. You will find sections on idioms, phrasal verbs, pronunciation, and slang. The site also provides practice quizzes on irregular verbs, proper use of prepositions, and other troublesome English issues.

   www.eslcafe.com

2. *To Learn English:* This site provides free material on issues that face ESLs. You will find American slang with translations as well as helpful vocabulary. The reading comprehension section provides a news story and then tests your comprehension in a short quiz.

   www.tolearnenglish.com

3. *Education resources on the Internet:* The Digital Education Network, Ltd., operates this site that offers courses in English. Some elements are free; however for others, you will pay a fee.

   www.edufind.com

4. *English coursework:* Englishsite provides a list of coursework available to internationals or those interested in becoming certified to teach English. Coursework includes training for the TOEFL (Test of English as a Foreign Language).

   www.englishsite.com

5. *Accent management:* Hundreds of listings on the Internet (go to Google and enter "accent reduction") lead to sites of companies specializing in accent management or reduction. Many universities also offer courses to make accents more understandable for American audiences. Two companies that you may want to consult are Atlanta Accent Management, Inc., www.atlantaaccentmanagement.com/ and ESL.net/.

RESOURCE C
Bibliography

This bibliography serves both to acknowledge our sources and to provide readers with references for additional reading.

Adler, N., *International Dimensions of Organizational Behavior*, 4th ed., South-Western, 2002.

Andrews, D. C., *Technical Communication in the Global Community*, Upper Saddle River, NJ: Prentice Hall, 2001.

Babcock, L., and S. Laschever, *Women Don't Ask: Negotiation and the Gender Divide*, Princeton, NJ: Princeton University Press, 2003.

Bateson, M., *Composing a Life*, New York: Atlantic Monthly Press, 1990.

Beamer, L. and I. Varner, *Intercultural Communication in the Global Marketplace*, Boston: McGraw-Hill Irwin, 2001.

Cook, R. A., G. Cook, and L. Yale, *Guide to Business Etiquette*, Upper Saddle River, NJ: Prentice Hall, 2005.

De Ley, G., *International Dictionary of Proverbs*, New York: Hippocrene Books, 1998.

Ferraro, G., *The Cultural Dimension of International Business*, 4th ed., Upper Saddle River, NJ: Prentice Hall, 2002.

Glaser, C., and B. Smalley, *More Power to You: How Women Can Communicate Their Way to Success*, New York: Warner Books, 1995.

Goldin-Meadow, S., *Hearing Gesture: How Our Hands Help Us Think*, Boston, MA: Harvard University Press, 2004.

Gundling E., *Working GlobeSmart: 12 People Skills for Doing Business Across Borders*, Palo Alto, CA: Davies-Black Publishing, 2003.

Hall, E., and M. Hall, *Understanding Cultural Differences*, Yarmouth, ME: Intercultural Press, Inc., 1990.

Hindle, T., *Essential Managers: Negotiating Skills*, New York: D.K. Publishing, 1998.

Hoff, Ron, *I Can See You Naked*, Kansas City: Andrews and McMeel, 1992.

Kenton, S. B., and D. Valentine, *CrossTalk: Communicating in a Multicultural Workplace*, Upper Saddle River, NJ: Prentice Hall, 1997.

Knauer, K., "When America Went to War, American Women Went to Work," http://www.nationalparks.org/ProudPartners, accessed September 22, 2004.

Lewis, R. D., *When Cultures Collide*, London: Nicholas Brealey Publishing, 1999.

Moran, R., and W. Stripp, *Successful International Business Negotiations*, Houston, TX: Gulf Publishing Co., 1991.

Morrison, T., W. Conaway, and G. Borden, *Kiss, Bow, or Shake Hands: How to Do Business in Sixty Countries*, Holbrook, MA: Bob Adams, Inc., 1994.

Munter, M., "Cross-Cultural Communication for Managers," *Business Horizons*, May–June 1993, 69–76.

_____, *Guide to Managerial Communication*, 6th ed., Upper Saddle River, NJ: Prentice Hall, 2002.

Reynolds, S., and D. Valentine, *Guide to Cross-Cultural Communication*, Upper Saddle River, NJ: Prentice Hall, 2004.

Rosen, R., *Global Literacies: Lessons on Business Leadership and National Cultures*, New York: Simon & Schuster, 2000.

Strunk, W., and E. White, *The Elements of Style*, New York: Macmillan, 1995.

Tannen, D., *Talking from 9 to 5: Women and Men at Work*, New York: Quill, 2001.

Truss, L., *Eats, Shoots, & Leaves: The Zero Tolerance Approach to Punctuation*, New York: Gotham Books, Penguin Group, 2003.

Zelazny, G., *Say It with Charts*, New York: McGraw-Hill, 1996.

RESOURCE D

Suggested Novels About the U.S. Culture

Because literature can often reveal and clarify culture, the following works will help you learn about the American culture.

James Agee, *Death in the Family* and *Let Us Now Praise Famous Men*

Sherwood Anderson, *Winesburg, Ohio*

Paul Auster, *The New York Trilogy*

James Baldwin, *The Fire Next Time* and *Nobody Knows My Name*

Saul Bellow, *Dangling Man* and *Adventures of Augie March*

Truman Capote, *Breakfast at Tiffany's*

Willa Cather, *My Antonia* and *O Pioneers!*

Stephen Crane, *The Red Badge of Courage*

E. L. Doctorow, *Ragtime* and *Billy Bathgate*

Theodore Dreiser, *Sister Carrie*

Ralph Ellison, *Invisible Man*

Ralph Waldo Emerson, *Self-Reliance*

William Faulkner, *Light in August* and *As I Lay Dying*

F. Scott Fitzgerald, *The Great Gatsby*

Zane Grey, *The Last of the Plainsmen*

Nathaniel Hawthorne, *The Scarlet Letter* and *The House of the Seven Gables*

Ernest Hemingway, *Farewell to Arms* and *The Sun Also Rises*

Henry James, *Daisy Miller* and *The American*

Jack Kerouac, *On the Road*

Sinclair Lewis, *Babbitt* and *Main Street*

Jack London, *The Sea Wolf*

Norman Mailer, *An American Dream*

Herman Melville, *Moby Dick* and *Billy Budd*

Carson McCullers, *The Heart Is a Lonely Hunter* and *Member of the Wedding*

Joyce Carol Oates, *We Were the Mulvaneys*

Ayn Rand, *The Fountainhead* and *Atlas Shrugged*

Philip Roth, *American Pastoral*

Upton Sinclair, *The Jungle*

John Steinbeck, *Grapes of Wrath* and *Travels with Charley in Search of America*

Mark Twain, *The Adventures of Tom Sawyer* and *The Adventures of Huckleberry Finn*

Edith Wharton, *The Age of Innocence*

Thomas Wolfe, *Look Homeward, Angel* and *You Can't Go Home Again*

Richard Wright, *Native Son*

RESOURCE E

Suggested Films About the U.S. Culture

The cinema is a powerful medium to reveal culture. The following listing, although far from exhaustive, provides film titles that are useful in helping you learn about the United States.

All About Eve
All the President's Men
American Graffiti
Annie Hall
Apocalypse Now
Auntie Mame
Barbarians at the Gate
The Best Years of Our Lives
Born Yesterday
Citizen Kane
A Civil Action
Cold Mountain
Cool Hand Luke
Daughters of the Dust
The Deerhunter
Friendly Persuasion
Giant

Glory
The *Godfather* Series
Gone With the Wind
Guess Who's Coming to Dinner
High Noon
In America
Inherit the Wind
It's a Wonderful Life
Julia
Man in the Grey Flannel Suit
Marty
*M*A*S*H*
Meet Me in St. Louis
Midnight Cowboy
Mr. Smith Goes to Washington
On the Waterfront
Other People's Money
Patton
Showboat
Spellbound
To Kill a Mockingbird
Twelve Angry Men
West Side Story
You Can't Take It With You

Index